WHAT
MATTERED
MOST

WHAT MATTERED MOST

A Memoir

TY HERNDON

with David Ritz

DEYST.
An Imprint of WILLIAM MORROW

DEYST.

"Journey On"
Written by Caleb Collins + Ty Herndon
Publishing: Sunset Gallery Music, Journey On Publishing

"The Rest of My Life"
Written by Matthew S. Garringer + Ty Herndon
Publishing: Sunset Gallery Music, Journey On Publishing

"Don't Pass Me By"
Written by Caleb Collins, Joel Lindsey + Ty Herndon
Publishing: Sunset Gallery Music, Bridge Building Music, Hefton Hill Music, Journey On Publishing

"I Cried Out"
Written by Reba Rambo-McGuire, Dony McGuire + Ty Herndon
Publishing: He Gave Me Music, Journey On Publishing

"God or the Gun"
Written by Jamie Floyd, Erik Halbig, Hector Montenegro + Ty Herndon
Publishing: Jamie Floyd Music, Journey On Entertainment

"Till You Get There"
Written by: Jamie Floyd, Erik Halbig, Jimmy Thow + Ty Herndon
Publishing: Anthem Entertainment/Hertz So Good Publishing, Jamie Floyd Music, Journey On Entertainment

All songs used by permission

All photos courtesy of the author.

Without limiting the exclusive rights of any author, contributor or the publisher of this publication, any unauthorized use of this publication to train generative artificial intelligence (AI) technologies is expressly prohibited. HarperCollins also exercise their rights under Article 4(3) of the Digital Single Market Directive 2019/790 and expressly reserve this publication from the text and data mining exception.

WHAT MATTERED MOST. Copyright © 2026 by Ty Herndon. All rights reserved. Printed in the United States of America. No part of this book may be used or reproduced in any manner whatsoever without written permission except in the case of brief quotations embodied in critical articles and reviews. For information, address HarperCollins Publishers, 195 Broadway, New York, NY 10007. In Europe, HarperCollins Publishers, Macken House, 39/40 Mayor Street Upper, Dublin 1, D01 C9W8, Ireland.

HarperCollins books may be purchased for educational, business, or sales promotional use. For information, please email the Special Markets Department at SPsales@harpercollins.com.

hc.com

FIRST EDITION
Designed by Patrick Barry
Library of Congress Cataloging-in-Publication Data has been applied for.
ISBN 978-0-06-336010-5

26 27 28 29 30 LBC 5 4 3 2 1

AUTHOR'S NOTE

When I started writing this book a couple of years ago, I thought I was just putting my story on paper. Turns out, I was facing my past—the good, the bad, and the downright ridiculous—and having a long, overdue conversation.

There are some tough stories in here, sure, but there's also a whole lot of joy and humor. Because life's not just about surviving the storm. It's about dancing in the puddles afterwards.

You'll meet people who changed me. Some loved me when I couldn't love myself. Some challenged me, some hurt me, and some walked away. And every one of them helped me become the man I can be today. Whether we still talk or not, my heart carries gratitude for each of them. They all played a part in keeping me alive long enough to figure out who I was meant to be.

As I wrote, I found myself smiling remembering moments that gutted me at the time. I found forgiveness where I never thought I would. And in riffling through the chaos of my past, I found peace.

Music has always been my way of telling the truth three minutes at a time. But this book gave me the space to tell it all. So, to the friends, the family, the cowriters, the believers, the ones who hung in there—and even the ones who couldn't—thank you. You're part of this story whether you know it or not.

And to you, the reader, buckle up. This is a wild ride, full of detours. But love was always my guide. Ultimately, love saved me.

With deep gratitude,
Ty

CONTENTS

	Preface: A Word from a Ghost	ix
1:	Long Walk Home	1
2:	The Revival	3
3:	"Your Life Has Just Begun"	11
4:	Shampoo Boy	17
5:	Big Moves	23
6:	The Big Break	31
7:	Contest Crazy	43
8:	Rape	47
9:	Life and Death	57
10:	Meet Miss North Carolina	61
11:	Meet the Cowboy	65
12:	Meet the Drag Queen	71
13:	"You Need to Meet Cher"	81
14:	What Mattered Most	87
15:	Caught	95
16:	Instant Rehabilitation	107
17:	"Death, Be Not Proud"	113
18:	Living in a Moment	117
19:	Hollywood	127

20:	"The Good Life"	137
21:	"Help Me Make It Through the Night"	145
22:	Miss Peggy and the Coffin	151
23:	"I Am a Fake"	155
24:	*Walk the Line*	159
25:	"I Will Not Set Foot in Your Church"	165
26:	Right About Now	171
27:	Restoration Herndon	177
28:	Matt	185
29:	"Lies I Told Myself"	189
30:	Out!	193
31:	*God and the Gay Christian*	201
32:	Trouble in Paradise	205
33:	The Myth of Monogamy	209
34:	Armageddon	213
35:	The Beauty of Flowers	219
36:	Melting Icebergs	227
37:	"Some Enchanted Evening"	233
38:	Letting Go	247
39:	The Now	251
	Acknowledgments	255

PREFACE

A Word from a Ghost

DAVID RITZ

I USUALLY ADHERE to the rule that restrains the ghostwriter from raising his voice. The ghostwriter's job is to channel the voice of someone else. I'm breaking the rule because, in this case, the someone else is so exceptional that I feel the need to introduce him. Working intimately with him for several years now has made my perspective unique. And though I've ghosted dozens of books over seven decades, I've never encountered a character with Ty Herndon's irrepressible energy.

At the family Christmas party, I was seated on a couch next to Miss Peggy, Ty's mother, when she said, "Look at my son. He never stops."

"He never stops" is the mantra. "He never stops" is the key.

Ty is a commanding presence. You can't ignore him. He's incurably charming, endearingly engaging. And he's in constant motion. He's bringing in the food, he's attending to each guest, he's cleaning up plates, he's telling stories, he's entertaining, he's laughing, he's singing, he can't sit down or take a break or stop working to make sure everyone feels welcome and comfortable. He's a man who must see to the needs of others. Always others before himself.

In our endless discussions about his life, he might settle down for a second, but then he'll jump up, he'll be driving his truck, he'll be scrubbing the floors or folding the laundry or emptying the garbage or feeding the dog—all while answering the toughest questions I can devise. When the questions trigger him, as they often do, he'll grow more frenetic but never hostile. He'll never say "You're pushing me too far" or "Enough is enough." In his freneticism, he'll keep the dialogue going but at the same time wash every dish in the sink or start baking biscuits. Just as he'll never stop cooking or cleaning or sewing, he'll never stop trying to get to the bottom of the biggest question of all: Who am I?

Ty's a searcher. His appetite for self-knowledge is insatiable. He harbors big spiritual ambitions. He wants to expand. He's curious to a fault. While standing in line at Starbucks or shopping at Costco, he elicits stories from strangers who—just like that—treat him like a lifelong friend. He's pleased to be recognized by a fan, but even more pleased to generate goodwill from someone he just met. He wants to win over the world.

His story moves like Ty does: fast. He's in a hurry to let you know what he's been through. Just listen to him . . .

Ty and his coauthor, David Ritz, in 2024.

WHAT
MATTERED
MOST

CHAPTER 1

LONG WALK HOME

I'D LOVE FOR you to love me. I'd love for you to see me as just a good ol' country boy without a care in the world. I'd love for you to feel my evangelical energy, the spirit I first felt as a little boy. My energy runneth over. Glory Hallelujah! I'd love for that spirit to make me look good. Yet—and this is the scary part—this book will definitely *not* make me look good. This book is going to make me look confused, afraid, terrified, lost, and dishonest.

To tell my story truthfully, I need to be honest about my decades of dishonesty. I need to dredge up old traumas. I need to revisit darkness from my past. I need to let you know how I repeatedly messed up after promising never to mess up again. I want to leave out all the times that I fell back into destruction. I'm embarrassed by how long I believed I had it together when, in fact, I was falling apart. I'm afraid you'll give up on me and just put the book down.

Humiliation, shame—I want none of those feelings, and yet those are feelings I know very well and emotions I need to own up to. If I don't, they'll haunt me forever.

It's a long walk home to the truth.

This is the task I've taken up—documenting that walk. Presenting myself as I was and as I am. A broken man. A healed man who got broken only to heal again. A cycle and a circle that went on for a very long time.

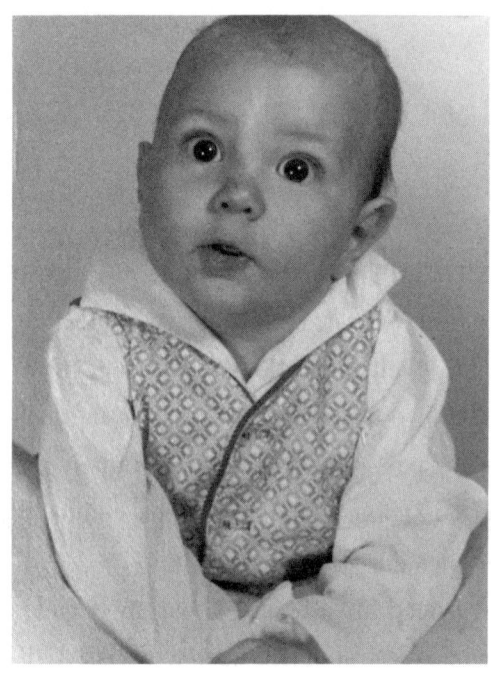

Ty at six months old.

CHAPTER 2

THE REVIVAL

THE CALMNESS OF a moonlit night.

The feeling of being protected in the bosom of a close-knit family.

I felt safe, excited, and loved.

On May 2, 1972, I—Boyd Tyrone Herndon—was ten years old, not only a happy and bright birthday boy but, in my mind, the best little boy in all the world. I was set to both sing and testify at a tent revival.

Growing up in rural Alabama in a town called Butler, just east of the Mississippi border, I embraced all that was comfortable about the Deep South. The friendliness. The warmth. The easy pace of country living. The certainty of faith.

Faith in God was no abstract idea. It was my emotional reality, and it had me jumping up and down in full-on praise and worship whenever I stepped foot into church. I immediately felt God's presence. That feeling didn't emerge from books or preaching. It was always there. It was mystical. I was a blood-washed believer who thrived on God's love. And a tent revival brought that love into technicolor.

My faith, and every contour of my childhood, was shaped by the women who reigned over my family.

My grandmother Myrtle had four daughters: my mother, Peggy; my beloved aunts Lily Pearl and Benny Sue; and Aunt Greta, the secret daughter from Grandma's never-discussed first marriage. I say "secret" because I didn't know about Grandma's earlier marriage till later in life. Greta was wide-open. And her name is pronounced "Greeta," with a long *e*.

I adored all these women, and they adored me.

Grandma Myrtle was the Great Matriarch. She was a force of nature who had chartered the Calvary Baptist Church in her living room. Soon there was a freestanding sanctuary. Grandma also hosted a radio program, *The Variety Hour*, featuring her daughters—Mom's sisters and besties. Grandma loved the Lord and music, and she let the world know it. She went to heaven with her acoustic Gibson in her lap.

Decades before she passed, Myrtle had prepared me for my life's work. At five years old, I was placed on a Coca-Cola box so I could reach the mic and sing on her radio show. Every Saturday night the family listened to the *Grand Ole Opry* and the gospel hour *Jubilee* on Myrtle's radio. Loretta, Tammy, Merle, Conway Twitty, the Statlers,

The Todd sisters: Lily Pearl, Benny Sue, Greta Lanelle, and Peggy Geanie.

Bill Monroe's bluegrass gospel—these were the artists who got my blood to boiling, even as a kid.

Mom and Grandma said I was a natural. By age nine, I knew my life's duty was to carry my grandmother's and aunts' dreams to become gospel artists beyond the bounds of our rural community.

When I was called to the pulpit, I proudly gave my testimony both in word and song.

"I may be young," I said, "but God lives in me."

My main teacher, though, was neither Mom nor Grandma. It was Aunt Benny Sue, who taught me to sing and play piano. She also tutored me in scripture. Aunt Benny Sue, along with her husband, Uncle Al, attended the Gilbertown Pentecostal Church of God. Gilbertown was seventeen miles down the road from Butler, but it felt like another world.

The division between the Pentecostals and the Baptists was deep. As a church boy, I had big love for all houses of worship, but I could tell the difference. I went to the Baptist Church, but the Baptists were a little staid. Unlike the Baptists, the Pentecostals let kids participate in everything. And everything excited me—women waving their hands, folks catching the Holy Ghost, talking in tongues and running the aisles. The church's hyperenergetic spirit matched mine. The Pentecostals got me high on the Holy Spirit. And if kids got tired after five hours of praising and worshipping, they'd fall asleep under the pews, but not me. My energy wouldn't let me rest.

I was a country boy, steeped in scripture and gospel music. But as for the wider world, I didn't have a clue. And back on that late spring night in 1972, on my birthday, I couldn't wait to testify and sing at the revival in the enormous tent.

In my young mind, singing and preaching went together. I had the ability to quote scripture at length and explain its meaning—how the good news of the Gospel was that there is no death; love lives forever. I liked hearing myself sound older than I was. And, of course, I also liked hearing my singing voice; I liked the feeling that came with effortlessly carrying a melody and singing in tune. I loved praising God in word and song. On this particular night, I was sure to get plenty of praise. I was with Grandma Myrtle and Aunt Benny Sue and her family. We drove far out into the countryside to a spot where dozens of cars and pickups were arriving. When I saw the oversized tent, my heart started hammering. The bigger the crowd, the more souls to save. The evening breeze was cool and refreshing. The sky was clear.

We were walking inside the tent when I saw the usher, a super-strict Bible thumper. He was standing at the entrance of the tent, where he'd confronted two teenage girls. To my amazement, he was refusing to allow them in.

"Go home and put on dresses!" he yelled. The young ladies were wearing pants.

"Who cares?" asked one of the girls.

"God does!" he boomed.

When they tried to push their way past him, he struck them both on their heads with his Bible. The Bible thumper actually thumped them with his Bible! The girls ran from the tent. I wanted to say something. Wasn't the girl right? Did God really care about how we dressed? And wasn't it a sacrilege to use the Bible as a weapon? But I was a child. I knew to stay silent.

We walked inside where, because I was performing, we were ushered to seats in the first row. There were at least two hundred people in attendance.

Shortly after the service began, I was called up to sing a hymn in the manner of those Southern artists who had inspired me—Johnny Cook, The Happy Goodmans and the Hinsons. I then preached briefly on John 13:35, which says, "By this all people will know that you are my disciples, if you have love for one another." That passage was a beacon for me. Its meaning was plain. Everyone should love everyone. That was my understanding of Christ.

My singing was greeted with thunderous applause. So was my preaching. I was a local favorite and loved the attention coming my way. While I was up there, though, I saw that the celebrated minister in charge of this revival—I'll just call him Preacher—was looking at me with unusual intensity. I wondered why. When I sat down and he came to the makeshift pulpit to preach, I found out.

Preacher possessed great self-assurance. His posture was correct. His eyes were ice blue, his black wavy hair perfectly in place. His wide shoulders and broad chest gave him the look of a prizefighter. He wore gray pleated trousers and a white open-collared shirt with the sleeves rolled up to his elbows. His arms were hairless. His voice was powerful. He spoke in a thick Southern drawl.

Preacher began by saying, "The New follows the Old, and so it is with the Word that contains God's unalterable laws. You cannot fathom the New Testament without abiding by the Old. Please open your Bibles to Leviticus."

After some general remarks about how this third book of Moses focuses on God's demand that we avoid sin, he asked us to look at Leviticus 18 and 20.

He quoted chapter 18, verse 22: "You shall not lie with a male as with a woman; it is an abomination."

Then chapter 20, verse 13: "If a man lies with a male as with a woman, both of them have committed an abomination; they shall surely be put to death; their blood is upon them."

Then Preacher suddenly came from behind the pulpit and stood right in front of me. I didn't know what to make of it. I was frightened and shocked.

He pointed at me, his finger inches from my face, and said, "Homosexuality is not only ungodly but a sickness that corrupts the soul. Do you hear me?"

He was speaking directly to me.

Why?

Others shouted out, "We hear you, brother!"

If he hadn't used Leviticus to define homosexuality, I'm not sure I would have understood the word. I had never said it. It appeared in no book that I had read. No one in my family had uttered it. And now the word struck me dumb.

I stayed silent, frozen with the secret knowledge that, during my early years of puberty, I had harbored romantic attraction toward other boys, feelings I had suppressed. Not a soul knew, and yet Preacher continued pointing at me as though he could read my mind.

As his voice grew louder, he drew so close that I could smell his breath. I was afraid he would demand that I stand, face the congregation, and confess. If that happened, I was prepared to lie. I would profess allegiance to the Old Testament. I would swear on his Bible that I was not a homosexual.

"And if you do have homosexual thoughts," he bellowed, continuing to gaze into my eyes, "I say repent now, repent before it is too late, repent or face eternal damnation."

He then paused and pointed at me again. I couldn't catch my breath. Time stopped. I thought I might pass out. I tried to pretend that this was all a dream. When that didn't work, I prayed for a hole to open in the ground so I could disappear and never be seen again. I broke into a sweat. My hands began to shake.

Seeing that I was about to crater, Aunt Benny Sue put her arm around me. If she hadn't, I would have collapsed. I couldn't imagine that she knew my secret, but that didn't matter. She saw her nephew crumbling before the Preacher's ferocious accusations and knew he needed protection.

His tirade went on for what seemed like forever. In truth, it was no more than twenty minutes, but in those twenty minutes my tender heart suffered a life-altering blow. My relationship to God and God's Word collapsed. I stood accused. I stood condemned. I wanted to die.

When the service was over, I was shaking all over. I saw Aunt Benny Sue make a beeline for Preacher. I couldn't hear what she said, but I could see that she was furious. She was no doubt scolding him for shaming her nephew in public. His response was to look the other way.

The secret stayed locked inside me. It festered and corroded my heart, defining me for longer than I want to remember.

I have lived and relived that night ten thousand times. I hated Preacher longer than I have ever hated anyone. I hated him with such force that I made myself sick. I hated him until I realized that he was probably haunted by the same secret that haunted me. Was he enraged by what he called "a demon desire" because that was the very desire that he could never exorcise? Or was he just jealous of all the attention I got right before he took the stage?

I'll never know.

All I do know is that, in the name of God, he crushed my spirit that night. I now understand that Preacher, like all of us, had his own story. He had a mother, a father, a history that made him who he was. I never saw him again. He may be dead. He may have gone the way of Elmer Gantry or Jimmy Swaggart. Maybe he's in prison, or maybe he's making millions leading a megachurch that pushes the gospel of prosperity. It doesn't matter. Like every soul, he deserves compassion, the kind of compassion that I was unable to offer myself for a very long time. At that moment, in that tent, in that makeshift tabernacle of God, I felt as though my life was over.

CHAPTER 3

"YOUR LIFE HAS JUST BEGUN"

THAT'S WHAT MOM told me when she learned from her sister Benny Sue what had happened in the tent. Mom didn't give a hoot that I was a different kind of kid. Now I know that she sensed that difference had to do with sexual orientation, but even that was fine with Mom. She saw that I was hyper and—until the incident in the tent—happy. She liked that I had energy to burn. She understood that energy could serve me well.

As a Southern lady, Miss Peggy had natural charm. She was quick to laugh, quick to invite all my friends to our dinner table. She was the salt of the earth. She took delight in raising me; she showered attention on me, but she also knew when to leave me alone. She possessed maternal wisdom that saved me at moments when I was close to self-destruction. Even as she warned me, she never judged me. Nothing threw her. She walked through life with a calmness that counterbalanced my restless drive.

Grandma Myrtle and my aunts also offered me great understanding and acceptance. I was their golden boy with a golden voice.

After the Preacher shamed me, I stopped preaching but never stopped singing. I kept on singing in Aunt Benny Sue's Pentecostal church. Singing was my sacred gift; one that, no matter the circumstances, made me feel worthy. When I was singing, I never felt shame. When I wasn't, shame was my constant companion. I always wondered whether my father was ashamed of me.

Dad was a man's man. He was distant, especially with me. Throughout my childhood, he never said, "Son, I love you." Never said, "Son, I'm proud of you."

Much later I learned that Dad had suffered as a child. His mother, Grandma Inez, was sickly and bedridden from birthing nine children on a rural farm. She died when Dad, her youngest child, was twenty. My grandfather was indifferent and cold to my father. Coldness was Dad's inheritance. Mom said Dad loved me, and I believed her, but I never felt it.

Before the trauma of the tent revival, I had lived an idyllic childhood. Me, Mom, Dad, and my little sister, Alicia, lived in one of the two double-wide trailers on the farm owned by Mom's folks, Grandma Myrtle and Grandpa Heyward. Aunt Lily and her family lived in the trailer next door.

L: Ty's father as a young man, Wesley Boyd Herndon, holding Ty as a baby. R: Boyd Herndon as a young man.

It was a land of vegetation and livestock. Corn, black-eyed peas, soybeans, and butterbeans; horses, pigs, and chickens. The fragrance of wildflowers, the stink of manure, the scent of fresh soil after a rainstorm. Rainbows you could practically touch.

The city of Butler was small-town America—a courthouse, a movie theater (where I saw my first movie, *101 Dalmatians*), a funeral home, a paper mill, a Chinese restaurant, a general store owned by Grandpa Heyward, and a drugstore where Mom worked. The Butler Hotel had a restaurant with a daily special. I liked Tuesday's: fried green tomatoes, fried chicken, turnip greens, and cornbread and biscuits.

Mom was a Barbara Mandrell–short lady with a pretty face and a fetching figure. She met Dad in an odd way. It happened because she'd been dating a man named Al who worked with Boyd Herndon, my dad-to-be, at the local paper mill. Al wasn't her type, so he fixed her up with Boyd. Boyd *was* her type. Al turned out to be Aunt Benny Sue's type, and after marrying Benny Sue, he became Uncle Al.

My folks' first date was at the county fair across from Grandpa's general store. In the middle of a huge field, a two-engine plane set down and, to everyone's delight, out walked Cowboy Copas, a big-time country singer, to play his big hits "Candy Kisses" and "'Tis Sweet to Be Remembered." He then climbed back into the plane and flew away as mysteriously as he had appeared. Peggy and Boyd couldn't help but believe Cowboy Copas had come to Butler to memorialize their first date. It was a good omen. (Or was it? This was the same Cowboy Copas who, later, died in a plane crash with Patsy Cline.)

My parents' courtship was red-hot. Within two months, they were married. Mom figured that she and Dad would move to Panama City, Florida—his hometown—but that never happened. Dad stayed in Butler because the pay at the Champion International Paper mill was good. He eventually became a maintenance supervisor.

Boyd Herndon was a big man who drove a big truck. He was a looker—six-foot-two with a beautiful thick mustache. He exuded strength and unfettered masculinity. When he walked around in his underwear that revealed too much, Mom would say, "These kids are too old to see you like that. Put on some pants." Let's just say my dad had nothing to be ashamed of.

By age ten, my sexuality had set in. Not that I'd tell a soul—and not that I'd even admit it to myself—but it was there. The desire frightened me. I did all I could to suppress it. My friend Dean told me that if I rubbed my dick long enough, I'd have a "celebration." So, I went right home and celebrated. I loved it but also hated it. It felt so shameful that I promised God I would never do it again. Then, ten minutes later, I was off celebrating for a second time. And then a third. The pattern set in.

Due to the excruciating trauma he suffered as a child, my dad had a drinking problem later in life, but booze never stopped him. Booze never stopped him from working. He was also Mr. Fixit and Mr. Mechanic. Somehow Dad built a '65 Mustang out of a VW bug.

Our father-son moments were few but memorable. Dad was set on teaching me how to hunt deer. He showed me a "deer stand," a contraption that looked like a treehouse. It was five feet off the ground and could hold two or three men. He placed it close to a grassy knoll where deer liked to graze. This was doe season, when the deer population doubled. Dressed in camouflage, Dad and nine-year-old me stepped up into the deer stand. We each had a 20-gauge shotgun. Our position was perfect.

"Like shooting fish in a barrel," said Dad.

When I showed hesitancy, Dad reminded me that this was not sport. We ate everything we killed. And besides, the law had imposed a limit: We could slaughter no more than three does.

Dad's first shot was in the air, causing the deer to scatter and making it easy to target them.

"Go on," said Dad.

I wanted to go on. I wanted to make him proud by killing at least one deer. I wasn't innocent. I had eaten deer meat. But eating deer was different from shooting them. I'd never murdered a living thing before. It didn't help that I had seen *Bambi*. Deer are adorable, the sweetest creatures on God's green earth.

These thoughts paralyzed me. I couldn't pull the trigger. I jumped out of the deer stand and screamed to the deer: *"Run! Get outta here before we kill you!"*

As the deer ran back into the woods, Dad was too disgusted with me to take another shot.

"Why did you do that?" he asked.

I had no answer.

"Let's just go home," he grunted.

On the long walk back, he stayed silent, but I felt his disappointment. I'd blown the chance to bond with my father.

We did bond over carpentry, though. I was still a preteen when Dad taught me how to sketch designs and build big pieces of furniture. Turned out that I had inherited his talent. I liked working with wood and got satisfaction from crafting a couch, bed frame, or love seat. I liked how Dad's rustic designs fit his personality. Slowly I got to the point where I could make furniture designs of my own.

Dad also introduced me to the rodeo. After Grandma Myrtle's radio show, the rodeo was the second venue where I sang for the public. During intermission I boldly walked to the mic dressed in my cowboy gear and belted out Glen Campbell's "Wichita Lineman." Big ovation for the little kid who sang with a manly voice.

But I did more than sing at the rodeo. I won a bunch of pig-wrestling contests. I was hoping that might merit a hug from Dad, but no such luck.

It didn't matter; I still loved the rodeo. Loved watching those cowboys ride the steers and work their fancy rope moves. I had crushes on many of those men. I didn't know it yet, but they were just my type. I loved how they looked in their tight Wranglers.

I'm amazed that today Gay Rodeo is an actual thing.

* * *

I was eleven when I entered a music talent contest at school. The organizers put me in the kids' category. I didn't like that. The kids were bush league. I wanted to be in the big league because I had a big voice. My confidence came from church, where I never failed to stir the congregation. Now, at school, I knew I could take on anyone and everyone.

And I did—thanks to Mom, who persuaded the judges to group me with the adults. Aunt Benny Sue accompanied me on piano as I sang "Teddy Bear Song," a country hit by Barbara Fairchild with a childlike melody and grown-up lyrics about an illicit love affair. I was good enough to win second prize, $175. Dad made me put most of it in the bank, but I got to use some of it to purchase records by Elvis Presley, Marty Robbins, and Susan Raye. Winning that prize let me shine.

The shine felt great, but my secret sexual stirrings kept getting stronger. What was I to do about those stirrings? How could I hide them?

CHAPTER 4

SHAMPOO BOY

AT AGE THIRTY-TWO, I had a number one hit on the country charts and found myself backstage at the Grand Ole Opry talking to Tammy Wynette. She was near the end of her storied career.

"Miss Tammy," I said, "I can't tell you what this moment means to me. Not only do I relate to your music, I relate to you as a hairdresser. I come from a family of hairdressers."

"Well, bless your heart," she said. "You do know I renew my cosmetology license my every year."

"Why is that, Miss Tammy?"

"Just in case this music thing doesn't work out."

We both laughed and started exchanging stories. Along with Mississippi, Miss Tammy called Alabama home and knew all about Butler. She wanted to hear about how I got caught up in hairdressing.

"My aunts taught me," I said. "They taught me to do all the Pentecostal hairdos."

That got her to open up her arms for a hug. I went in but made sure that the hugging wouldn't mess up her hair.

After that night, I went home too excited to sleep.

***

On a Saturday afternoon I might go hunting or fishing with Tommy, my cousin and best friend. Tommy was Aunt Benny Sue's son, the same aunt who had a mini beauty salon in her house. It was nothing more than an oversize utility closet. After catching a few catfish for dinner, I decided to head over to Aunt Benny Sue's for two reasons: First, everyone was there singing songs and praising the Lord, and second, I liked getting my hands wet. When Aunt Benny Sue said, "If you're gonna be in here, you gotta have a job," I willingly became Shampoo Boy.

I loved washing the wigs pinned to Styrofoam heads. But that day I got to climb up on the stool and soap up the hair of a living lady. As my little hands furiously worked up the suds, Aunt Benny Sue broke into "Have Thine Own Way, Lord." I joined in. The lady in the chair joined in. So did the holy spirit.

From Aunt Benny Sue's I ran over to Grandma Myrtle's. Grandma's hairdo was Patsy Cline–teased, curled in front and back. She wore

Ty's childhood best friend and first cousin, Tommy.

black block high heels. Stay out of Myrtle's way, because Myrtle ran her kitchen like a military operation. She also ran the general store and worked at the Vanity Fair factory as a seamstress sewing brassieres and buttons on shirts.

Grandma Myrtle's greatest talent was culinary. She never used a recipe. Her approach was "a pinch and a holler"—a pinch of your ingredients and holler when you think it's cooked. Oh, I loved watching her prepare chicken and dumplings! While singing "How Great Thou Art" or "All Is Well with My Soul," she'd take a white twin sheet, throw it out so the air would catch it, and let it land on the table. Then she'd roll out the flour with a tea glass—no rolling pin for her—before cutting it up into squares, sprinkling pepper on it, and, with lightning speed, dropping those dumplings into a giant pot of boiling rue, where, together with the hand-shredded strips of chicken, they'd simmer for two hours.

When I wandered in to take a whiff, she'd say, without a hint of humor, "Open that lid, Tyrone Herndon, and you'll lose a hand."

Grandma taught all her grandsons to cook because she was sure that would make us better husbands. She had that right. The woman was so fierce that even in her eighties she was selling a vat of chicken and dumplings for fifty dollars and her famous black-and-white cake with caramel icing for twenty-five dollars. Myrtle was a woman of many talents who adored her daughters but had little use for their husbands—and was quick to let them know.

Those husbands, starting with Dad, were all about control. Now I view them as men with deep insecurities. As a child, I viewed them with fear. Each and every one of them lorded over their women with an iron fist. My beloved mother, a strong, intelligent, and sensitive woman, was nonetheless cowed by her husband for almost all of their marriage. He was very controlling. If Mom was gone for more than thirty minutes, Dad had to know where she was. I learned not to trust my closest companion.

Uncle Al was filled with Pentecostal prejudice. Women were not allowed to wear pants or even their wedding rings. Aunt Benny Sue needed Uncle Al's permission to go anywhere. He was fun and funny and I loved him nonetheless.

Uncle Al's dad, Mr. Robinson, was the most dominant of them all. For example, I liked wearing my hair a little long and curly, but Mr. Robinson saw curly as girly and put me and four of my cousins into his truck and drove us straight to the barbershop.

"Give 'em all crew cuts," he told the barber.

I hated my haircut. I also hated being bullied. That happened in elementary school when a bully got the other kids to hold me down while he called me "singing boy." Even before the bully, I didn't want to go to school. After Mom forced me out of the car on the first day of first grade, I turned and chased after her, running nearly a mile back home. I already felt like I couldn't learn, and by second grade I had been placed in a special-needs class. I know now that I was suffering from severe ADHD, but no one knew of such things then. I just spent my school days unable to sit still and focus. Sometime later when Mom got a job as a secretary to the school principal, I was thrilled. To see her at school every day made me feel safe . . . until the bully came along.

I always cared about my looks, and now I looked like a horror show with a crew cut. I didn't want to be seen by anyone until I could get Mom to recut my hair at home. Only Mom could fix it. I ran down the hall to Mom's desk outside the principal's office. "Just hide in the utility closet," said Mom.

I squeezed into the closet, where a little later Principal Margaret Heaten discovered me hiding.

"Go back to class," she said.

"I can't," I whined. "My hair is ruined."

At that, she took out her paddle and whacked me twice on my behind. It stung, but even that didn't make me dislike her. In a world where women allowed men to dominate, no one dominated Principal Heaten. She was a powerhouse—and also a fan of my singing.

* * *

I was also an undiagnosed dyslexic, so I just had a hard time. I didn't learn my multiplication tables until I was in my thirties. So, thank God for music. Beyond music, I had little going for me. Girls didn't exactly flock to me. I sucked at sports, and, even worse, I had acne. Besides, it wasn't girls I wanted anyway. So I went to the woods, climbed up into my treehouse, shut my eyes, and pictured one of those rugged cowboys at the rodeo kissing me. Out of the woods, back home, I tried hard to envision myself married to a good Christian woman and living a good Christian life. My overwhelming aim was to be what the world wanted me to be: straight, strong, and normal.

Until Preacher called me out, I presumed my desire was invisible. But Preacher saw it. And named it. And condemned it. When he spelled out the conditions of God's love in those two explicit passages from Leviticus, I knew that I failed to meet those conditions. Therefore, God's love was no longer available to me.

I was a country boy without the intellectual sophistication to question a literal reading of the Bible. I didn't know the first thing about biblical interpretation.

I had been a prodigy, a wunderkind, a singer-preacher man-child destined to lead the masses to the joy of Christ. I was on fire for the Lord. Then the Preacher doused that fire with a hose of holy water.

He drowned my dreams with his judgment and interpretation of scripture. I was a queer pretending to be righteous. Queerness could never be righteous.

So, how to respond to my same-sex feelings?

Denial.

Denial was the only way forward. The alternative—to say I was gay—was inconceivable. Where I lived, no one did that. Where I grew up, there wasn't a single openly gay person. So, what could I do?

Not long ago, a friend told me about the classic autobiographical novel *Of Human Bondage* by W. Somerset Maugham. The hero is Philip Carey, who, as a boy, goes to sleep with the prayer that during the night God, who gives sight to the blind and life to the dead, will heal his clubfoot, the bane of his existence. When the sun rises and the boy reaches to touch his foot, the deformity is still there.

Maugham used the clubfoot as a substitute for what, in real life, was *his* bane: a severe stutter. But beyond being a stutterer, Maugham, a gay man, never came out. This is understandable, since in his time (1874–1965), practically no one in his world came out.

I relate to Maugham and his alter ego, Philip Carey. As a boy, I hated my sexual desires. I prayed for God to remove them. And when He didn't, when they not only intensified but transformed into a self-destructive addiction, I separated from my soul.

The division between who I was and who I wanted to be was devastating.

So, I adopted a double mind. I led a double life.

What lies ahead is a double-sided story, one part filled with love, the other filled with self-loathing.

CHAPTER 5

BIG MOVES

AT TWELVE, MY life changed for the better when we left Butler. Champion International Paper promoted Dad to a better job at their plant in Florence, Alabama. My folks bought a house in Decatur, an hour away from Florence. Decatur was hardly New York City, but in my eyes it might as well have been.

There was another reason why my folks wanted to leave Butler: dangerous racial tensions had been brewing there for years. Back in 1971, the Butler courthouse square was the scene of a civil rights demonstration. The issue was economic inequality in Choctaw County. During the protest, a white man killed a nineteen-year-old Black female protestor by driving over her with his car. He claimed it was inadvertent—that he was under attack. Others on the scene claimed otherwise. The man was charged but never prosecuted. The victim, Margaret Ann Knott, became a martyr. It took forty-six years, but a bridge was eventually named in her honor.

In the immediate aftermath of this tragedy, Reverend Ralph Abernathy, who had taken over the Southern Christian Leadership Conference after the assassination of Dr. Martin Luther King Jr., came to Butler to join the demonstrators. Along with 193 protestors,

Abernathy was jailed. The story went national, and suddenly our town was the focus of the civil rights struggle in America.

When this happened, we had moved from the double-wide trailer to a neighborhood called Green Acres. But we couldn't escape the underlying tension in Butler. Understandably, Blacks were enraged, not only by the death of Margaret Ann Knott but by the brutal oppression that had weighed upon them for hundreds of years.

My family was sympathetic to the protestors. My grandfather's general store was never targeted because of the goodwill he always extended to our Black neighbors. Mine was not a family mired in Southern racism. But when the offer of a better job in a different town came up, Dad grabbed it.

Goodbye, Butler; hello, Decatur.

* * *

Decatur represented a new start. Back in Butler, I had suffered with acne. In Decatur, my face started clearing up. My energy revived. As usual, music was why. No one likes being the new kid at school, but I dealt with that anxiety by joining the two-hundred-member choir. During the first semester of ninth grade, I got to sing solo on "He's Got the Whole World in His Hands."

Our choir director, Mr. Tommy Black, was a taskmaster and recognized something special about my talent. He often called me out in front of the class to sing a line. He knew how much I liked embellishing the melody, and he wasn't having it.

"No!" Mr. Black thundered. "I didn't say to sing it with a lick. Sing it straight!"

I sang it straight.

I played it straight too.

Back in 1969, the Stonewall Riots in New York's Greenwich Village had rocked the gay world. But in the Alabama of the mid-seventies, I knew nothing about Stonewall; I knew nothing about Greenwich Village; I was unfamiliar with the term "liberation"; I couldn't even say that I was in the closet because that metaphor was outside my vernacular. I did, though, develop a serious crush on a boy down the street, a great-looking guy who wore a leather jacket and flashed a friendly smile; I'll call him Boyfriend.

For two long summers, Boyfriend and I lived at Skate Castle at Funland Park, where I displayed my roller-skating skills. I had my own set of tricks, my own style, and loved singing along with the Bee Gees' "Stayin' Alive" and Donna Summer's "Bad Girls." Disco fever had hit Decatur, and I had it bad.

Boyfriend and I became more than roller-skating buddies. We rode our bikes beyond the cornfields outside Decatur. We found a secluded dell where we stretched out on our backs, breathed in the fresh air, and felt free. Boyfriend was just my type: cool and sexy and straight-acting.

Those afternoons were moments outside time. Before Boyfriend, I had been with another guy, who was sweetly effeminate and interested in giving but never receiving oral sex. With Boyfriend, it was reciprocal.

Boyfriend's family had little money. That prompted me to borrow from my dad so Boyfriend and I could go to the movies or skate together. Our relationship was easy. And though the world saw us as best buddies—two All-American guys—the world had no idea what was happening in that dell.

Boyfriend moved away before my first year of high school. That was both a heartbreak and a relief. I fooled myself into thinking that

I could focus on girls with him out of the picture. I realized that was going to be tough when I saw Burt Reynolds posing nude in an old copy of *Playgirl* magazine I found while I was babysitting for a family down the street. I also discovered Dad's reel-to-reel porn films. Thus began a crippling addiction to pornography.

All this was happening while Dad started attending the Walnut Grove Baptist Church. I went too and joined the Song Masters Gospel Quartet. Guilty over gay daydreams and secret porn watching, and full of a need to please Dad, I sang my heart out at Walnut Grove Baptist. I also started dating Candy, a fiery redhead who happened to be the preacher's daughter. Sweet Candy was the first girl I ever kissed. I might have made it to second base, but, God forbid, no further. Our friendship endured even when our short-lived romance ended. Candy left me for a big ol' handsome dude.

I was in my mid-teens when I lost my hetero virginity to an attractive girl who showed me the way in. It all happened on a plastic-covered couch while, in the nearby den, her elderly parents were snoring in their matching La-Z-Boy recliners. I enjoyed the act. The girl made me feel normal. I came home all aglow. Mom was in the kitchen, and Dad and I were at the dinner table.

"Go cut your fingernails before your mother gets in here," Dad demanded.

I asked why.

"There's a womanly smell under your fingernails," said Dad. "That smell is a dead giveaway."

I cut my fingernails, and when Mom served us dinner, she didn't detect a thing.

Dad gave me a knowing smile. The fragrance of a female on my hands made him happy.

Sex with a girl had me believing that I was bisexual. Yet in the late 1970s, the notion of bisexuality was foreign to the teenage culture of Decatur. Not a soul ever uttered that word, including yours truly.

Though the girl never said so, I'm sure she knew my secret. That turned out to be true with all the women I've slept with. My sexual energy is very strong. There have been times—and high school was one of them—when I used that excessive energy to bullshit myself, to get myself believing that I could take boys or leave them.

Yet while masturbating, I got off exclusively on fantasizing about straight-acting men. My desire for men never wavered. That desire was extreme and even obsessive. Was that normal? The fifteen-year-old Ty didn't think so. But the fifteen-year-old Ty had no gauge.

Like everyone else, I just wanted to fit in. That's where my dad went out of his way to help me. Real men rode motorcycles, so Dad gave me a 1965 F50 that he'd personally hand-painted. Dad also taught me how to build a dune buggy. Me and my buddies went mud bugging for hours at a time. If a buggy got stuck in the mud and broke down, no problem; I just built another one. I also had a Mustang, souped up by Dad, that gave me even more status. This was a moment when Dad definitely showed me affection—maybe because I had a girlfriend.

I had the gift of gab. I had a people-pleasing personality. I was friendly and funny and had no problem hanging out with the football players. The quarterback was my good buddy. Other boys, less masculine, were also pals. I could relate to everyone.

Girls piled into my Mustang. So did guys. It was a fun night out at the drive-in. Or it was miniature golf. Bowling, dancing, and skating. Acting like I didn't have a care in the world. I felt confident as the singing star at school and church. Yet my desire for dudes never abated. The distance between spiritual love and sexual love had me hopelessly confused.

But had you asked Tyrone Herndon, high school student, whether he felt confused, he'd deny it. Or if you asked Tyrone Herndon whether he was harboring self-hatred, he'd look at you like you were crazy.

Confusion and self-hatred were growing at an alarming rate.

Watch me roaring around town on my motorcycle. Watch me cruising in my Mustang. Watch me hanging out with the cheerleaders. Watch me hanging out with the nerds. I'm everything to everybody. Today is beautiful. Tomorrow will be even more beautiful. At school dances, I'm belting out Barry Manilow songs. During Christmas services, I'm tearing the roof off the church singing "Joy to the World"!

My secret same-sex suck-offs remain secret. Just boys being boys. I can stop those whenever I want. I'm normal. I'm going places.

Herndon family photo, 1980.

CHAPTER 6

THE BIG BREAK

A BREAK FROM normal life to theatrical life. A break from reality to fantasy, from regular folks to show folks. It was a bigger break than I could ever have imagined.

Opryland started calling to me when I was still in high school. Music director Tommy Black said that the theme park was recruiting singers. I'd been to Opryland before. It's where I first saw Kristin Chenoweth in "For Me and My Gal" at the Gaslight Theater.

The theme park, on the east end of Nashville, was massive: 120 acres, more than two million tourists a year, spectacular roller coasters like the Wabash Cannonball and the Rock n' Roller, the Country Bumpkin bumper cars, the Flume Zoom water ride, and every possible carnival game.

But mostly there was music. Opryland was a music dreamland. It was originally opened in the early seventies to introduce the brand-new four-thousand-seat seat Grand Ole Opry theater that replaced the original, housed in the Ryman Auditorium. Beyond country music, there was also bluegrass and R&B. "Rocking Around the Clock" was a fifties-style revue at the Jukebox Theater. A grand auditorium featured major musicals.

Opryland was a sprawling self-contained complex, a world of its own. It was where bright-eyed, eager-to-please eighteen-year-old Tyrone Herndon wanted to be. The audition was held in Birmingham, Alabama, eighty-five miles from Decatur. Mom said I could go, but only if my sister accompanied me. Alicia and I roared down the highway and arrived early. I sang, apparently to their satisfaction, because I was called back three times. After the third time, a week passed before I got the official word that I was in. The news got out quickly, and the principal made a congratulatory announcement to my entire high school.

But then another month came and went without a word. Mom called to ask whether they'd changed their minds.

"Heck no, Mrs. Herndon," said the man. "Ty needs to be in Nashville tomorrow for rehearsals."

Decatur to Nashville is 118 miles. It might as well have been 118 million miles. I was leaving black-and-white Kansas and entering Technicolor Oz.

If I burned up the highway, I could make it in ninety minutes. Starting my senior year, I made that trip every weekend. Things got hectic in a hurry. I ditched the Mustang for a more dependable Ford Fairlane. I was in such a fever that I got one speeding ticket only to get another ticket thirty minutes down the road.

I was originally hired because I could sing hymns. The plan was to put me in the Opryland Gospel Quartet, but then the departing member decided not to depart. That meant casting me in the brand-new show "Today's Country Roads." Three guys and three gals sang all the big country hits of 1980, from George Jones's "He Stopped Loving Her Today" to Crystal Gayle's "It's Like We Never Said Goodbye."

Singing before thousands of fans in an outdoor amphitheater was a rush I'd never felt before. I knew the songs. I could sing with conviction. I had the music part down pat. But things were moving so frantically that I could hardly catch my breath.

Running nonstop between Decatur and Nashville, I barely graduated high school. In fact, I shouldn't have received my degree, because, with a final grade of 59, I had failed algebra by a single point. I was heartbroken. Sensing this, my sweet teacher Mrs. White gave me the extra point out of the kindness of her heart.

The summer after graduation, I packed up and left home, ready to become an adult. I built my own furniture—a couch, chairs, tables, a bed frame—borrowed a pickup, and found a modest apartment in Music City.

I also received a one-year full-ride scholarship to Belmont College, a Christian school Minnie Pearl once attended. I signed up for a full load of courses and found myself running from classes in the mornings to Opryland in the evenings. I won first place in the college's freshman talent show singing Kenny Rogers's "Love the World Away." Student by day, entertainer by night, I was running a hundred miles an hour.

I couldn't complain about my Opryland salary—six hundred dollars a week. In fact, I couldn't complain about anything. In 1981, the year I turned nineteen, Roy Acuff invited me to sing at the Grand Ole Opry for what would be the first of my thirteen appearances in that hallowed hall.

My debut appearance turned into a double dream. Not only did I sing two songs but after performing the first one—Jack Greene's "There Goes My Everything"—I got to introduce Grandma Myrtle, who was in the audience along with my mom and aunts. She stood as the entire audience serenaded her with "Happy Birthday." As her eyes filled with tears, I thought of her local program back in Butler; I thought of the countless Saturday nights we had listened to the *Grand Ole Opry*. And now, praise God, I got to honor our family's grand matriarch.

If things were moving fast before, now the action was furious. Opryland had opened a huge new area called Grizzly Country where they built the Grizzly River Rampage, a rafting ride. Management decided to form a singing group called the Grizzly River Boys to hype this ride. Danny Gregg and Matt Davenport hired me as the trio's lead singer. We performed originals along with covers, like Ronnie Milsap's "Stranger in My House" and the Little River Band's "Who Made the Moon." Eagles songs, Jerry Lee Lewis songs, Creedence Clearwater Revival songs—we sang everything and became a sensation. Having outgrown the original Grizzly association, Danny and Matt changed our name to the Tennessee River Boys.

Amazingly, my name popped up in the *New York Times*: In an article about Opryland, their reporter wrote, "The buoyant new group called the Tennessee River Boys provides some of the finest of many hours of talented performers. Women flock to hear the handsome lead singer, Alabaman Ty Herndon, at the group's daily performances at the Gaslight Studio."

Women may have flocked to see me, but I was far more interested in the men. In mounting the musical *Show Boat*, Opryland built the front of an actual showboat that served as the background to a seven-story stage. Between the stage and the audience was a moat. This concert hall held a thousand seats. My focus became the male dancers—especially the man who played the captain. He was my age, Tom Selleck–tall and handsome, with a full mustache and a big, booming baritone voice.

The highlight of the show, though, was Kim Kennedy's grand entrance to "Can't Help Lovin' Dat Man." Her green gown was gorgeous. Her Ethel Merman–style delivery was riveting. The audience loved her. Once, when she stepped downstage a bit too far and fell into the moat, the audience was aghast, but not for long. She emerged from the water like Botticelli's *Venus* on the half shell, still singing the same note that she had sung before sinking. The crowd went wild.

I had to go backstage to congratulate her. It turned out that Kim Kennedy, nicknamed Muffy, was a love; she became one of my closest friends. After congratulating Kim, I wandered into the men's dressing room, where the fellas stood around buck naked except for their dance belts, devices that support the genitals. Those belts blew my mind.

The man who played the captain caught me eying the boys.

"I like those dance belts too," he said.

I was busted.

The captain was Wesley Ladell Meyers. We hit it off right away. That night we had dinner. He was a Mormon just back from his second missionary trip. He'd earned the sacred Mormon robes awarded only to the most devout. Like me, Wesley was excited by the pervasiveness of Opryland's queer culture. This was a first for us. Being brought up in homophobic settings, we'd both suffered similar confusion and guilt.

Wes was ahead of me. He had a boyfriend, another Mormon who also worked at Opryland. So, when the older male dancers pursued Wes, he said no. On the other hand, I said yes. I was a tall, strapping country boy. My world busted open. I didn't resist.

I was as horny as I was naïve. Those dancers couldn't get enough of me, and vice versa. It was never about romance. It was always hit-and-run, intoxicating but often deflating. Casual gay sex had my head spinning. Casual gay sex also made it impossible to deny my true sexual orientation.

My sister, Alicia, who'd always supported my career, came to Nashville and moved in with me while she started college. Spending time with her was a needed diversion from life at Opryland. At Christmas, Alicia and I liked driving out to the Nashville airport just to watch families reunite. They were strangers to us, yet they weren't. With bated breath, we waited for that moment when the grandchildren came running out into the arms of their grandparents. We loved hearing the screams of joy and seeing the hugs.

I thought living with Alicia might help rein in my promiscuity, but no one could have stopped me. Rumors began running riot.

"Three may keep a secret," said wise old Benjamin Franklin, "if two of them are dead." Attempts to hide my secrets always failed.

I can't claim that I was a victim of rumors. That's because the rumors were based on truth. The first rumor was started by an Opryland performer who also hailed from Decatur and knew a couple of the dancers with whom I'd had sex. He disapproved of homosexuality and started putting out the word about me: *Ty's queer.* Word may even have reached Mom and Dad. If it did, they said nothing and remained cool.

But I was not cool. I didn't want to be called a queer. I didn't want to *be* a queer. But I also didn't want to stop sleeping with these dancers. I adopted their attitude: *Do it and move on. Do it and don't get involved. Getting involved kills the thrill. The thrill is dependent on detachment. Don't catch a crush on anyone.*

Well, I did get a crush—a serious crush—on a six-foot-two singer and dancer with beautiful curly blond hair. He was an unapologetically closeted gentleman.

"I may be gay," he said, "but I'm not going to be gay with you. I'm never going to be gay with anyone."

We became great friends. And much to his credit, he was always trying to teach me about impulse control, a skill I lacked. My buddy had that skill, so much so that I'm not sure he ever had sex with a man. Suppression was his strategy for social survival.

I didn't have a strategy. I just had a longing. The longing soon transformed from wanting sex to wanting sex *and* romance. These one-night stands eventually left me lonely. And as my loneliness deepened, a pattern emerged: To stave off loneliness I sought more sex, which only made me lonelier. Any way you look at it, I was out of control.

At one point Opryland's entertainment director, John Haywood, who had originally hired me, called me to his office.

"Ty," he said, "you're a tremendous talent and have become a big attraction here at the park. I just want to make sure you're okay."

I wondered what he meant by that. Had he also heard rumors?

"I'm fine, Mr. Haywood. Just fine."

I almost asked why I wouldn't be fine, but I let the boss do the talking.

"You're young, Ty, and this entertainment business is a lot to handle. I just want to make sure you don't feel like this is too much for you."

What did he mean by that? Did he know about the sex? Was he saying that I had to stop fooling around with the dancers?

All I could think to say was, "I like singing here."

"And we like having you here, Ty. I'm just feeling a little protective. I don't want to see you get hurt."

Yes, I did feel that Mr. Haywood was looking out for me. But when he said "hurt," who did he think was hurting me?

It was a strange discussion that didn't last long. I didn't know what Mr. Haywood knew. All I knew was that the rumor mill kept churning. The only thing that may have stopped it was a surprising development.

I ran around seeing every single show at Opryland. I loved the big-time productions: *Bluegrass America. I Hear America Singing. Me and My Gal.* And especially *Country Music USA*, a historical look at the music I loved. I sat in the first row at the Roy Acuff Theater and, along with three thousand other fans, got goose bumps the minute the Tammy Wynette segment began.

A woman named Lisa played Tammy. Lisa was a knockout. Lustrous black hair. Legs for days. Seductive moves. Soulful voice. Dressed in sequined silver, Lisa walked down a long flight of purple-carpeted stairs as she sang Tammy's "Stand By Your Man." A pin spotlight framed her voluptuous figure. When she reached center stage, she hit the last note and held it until Jesus came back. Lights out.

The crowd went crazy, and when the lights switched on, Lisa and I locked eyes.

It was love at first sight.

When I went backstage to introduce myself, I was pleased that she already knew me from the Tennessee River Boys. We were both belters, both blood-washed gospel singers. We had a world in common. The chemistry was magical. I was convinced God had sent her to me.

Lisa and I fell in love. The romance was intense. I convinced myself that this wonderful woman was delivering me from secret sex. She was the one who would let me put this period of promiscuity behind me. We soon got engaged. I could see my future: Lisa would straighten me out. Lisa would deliver domestic bliss. We'd have a lovely home and three kids. We'd lead the normal, lovely life I had always desired.

So how do I explain the undoing of my relationship with Lisa?

Two words:

John Blaylock.

John also sang in *Country Music USA*. He had blond hair, dreamy blue eyes, and a come-hither smile. Like me, he hailed from small-town Alabama. He was funny as hell and loved the Lord. I found him irresistible, but I wasn't prepared to give up Lisa even as I fell in love with John.

But hadn't I just fallen in love with Lisa?

Yes. Romantic dates with Lisa on Saturday. Sex with John on Sunday.

Which was better?

Well, I was confused.

And my confusion came out in my behavior. I was crazy compulsive, calling Lisa one hour and then calling John the next. I was up and down, now ecstatic, now depressed. My mood swings were extreme. Happy about Lisa; unhappy about Lisa; unhappy about John; happy about John. I was down in the dumps or high in the heavens. A mental health pro would see this as bipolarity, but there were no mental health pros in sight.

Eventually John found out about Lisa. He wanted me all for himself, but because I wasn't willing to drop Lisa, John dropped me.

It didn't take long for Lisa to see that my interest in her was complicated. In the small world of Opryland, everyone knew everything. Lisa learned about my fling with John. And not long after John kicked me to the curb, Lisa followed suit. I couldn't blame her. I'd been a cad. It hurt me that I had so cruelly hurt her. It still haunts me to this day.

On the positive side, on a trip to Atlanta with John, we met Carl Peoples, also an Alabaman, also a singer, also a multitalented super-smart gay gentleman. John and Carl forged an unbreakable bond.

Carl wound up working at Opryland, where he became my lifelong friend. During every crisis in my life, Carl has been there for me. He had every reason to lose faith in me, but he never did. We were so close that at one point he moved in with my sister and mother in Nashville.

I've always had a group of gay brothers with whom I could be honest. But given my ambition and the tenor of the times, that honesty had limits. The double mind prevailed. And when my two relationships—one with Lisa and the other with John—fell into ruin, I was emotionally exhausted from straddling two worlds.

As my daddy used to say, straddle the fence too long and you'll bruise your balls.

I was tired of straddling. It was time to make a commitment. And who could question the wisdom of committing to God?

I returned to church—a Bible-based church that brought me back to my childhood. I needed to reconnect with my Pentecostal roots. I wanted to wave my arms to the heavens and praise Jesus. I needed reassurance. Let me rest in the bosom of the Lord.

So, I did. I attended Sunday services at the Cornerstone Assembly of God, a congregation close to Opryland. I answered the altar call one Sunday, declaring myself a sinner seeking spiritual cleansing. I promised God that I would give up all my same-sex shenanigans. I renounced my past and dedicated myself to Christ.

Christ soon led me to June, another beautiful brunette. I knew that to be true because I met June in church—June, who was as attracted to me as I was to her; June, who had a heart for God; June, whose fun-loving personality comforted and reassured me that she and I were meant for each other.

As with Lisa, I proposed within a month. June accepted. We were in perfect sync. We were in divine order.

Finally, I could put all the nonsense behind me.

Finally, life made sense.

Until it didn't.

Ty with his best man and best friend of more than forty years, Carl Peoples, at Ty and Alex's 2023 wedding.

Wes Meyers.

CHAPTER 7
CONTEST CRAZY

AMERICA'S INFATUATION WITH contests started in the 1930s on the radio with *Major Bowes Amateur Hour*. In the forties and fifties, Ted Mack took over and launched the careers of Pat Boone and Gladys Knight. *The Gong Show*, the TV show featuring both loony and legit talent, reigned in the seventies, but it really wasn't until *Star Search* emerged in the eighties that the craze rose to another level. Christina Aguilera, Justin Timberlake, Aaliyah, LeAnn Rimes, Rosie O'Donnell, Sinbad, Dave Chappelle . . . the list of performers who appeared on the television program hosted by Johnny Carson's sidekick, Ed McMahon, is long.

In 1983, the *Star Search* talent scouts came to Opryland and spent days listening to singers. They heard me with the Tennessee River Boys and chose me—without the other two band members. My trio-mates were hardly happy. They insisted that we appear on *Star Search* as a band. But the talent scouts wouldn't have it.

I asked entertainment director John Haywood for his opinion: Should I leave the group for a shot on the show?

"Out of all the Opryland singers," he said, "you were the only one chosen, Ty. You can't pass up this golden opportunity. I won't let you. I'm broadcasting the news to our entire community."

My mind sailed into orbit. I'd never ventured outside the states of Alabama and Tennessee. I'd never been on a plane. I'd never been to Hollywood. Suddenly I was about to be introduced to a national television audience by Johnny Carson's second banana.

June was supportive. She believed in my talent. We kissed goodbye, and I was off.

Hollywood didn't throw me. I stayed focused. I didn't go sightseeing. This was a time in my life when I didn't drink and had never taken drugs. I wanted no distractions. I wanted to win this thing, because I believed *Star Search* could change my life. I walked into that Sunset Boulevard TV studio feeling calm, cool, and collected.

The talent was divided into categories—comedy, modeling, etc. In music, the big ones were Bands and Male and Female Vocalist. No specific genre was designated. You just had to sing.

The studio audience didn't faze me. The cameras didn't faze me. I knew what to do when the red light came on. I had perfected my staple—the Gary Morris version of "The Wind Beneath My Wings."

Ty with fellow contestant and host, Ed McMahon, on *Star Search*.

I sang the song like I owned it. The four judges concurred. They gave me a perfect score. That night I called home and Mom cried with pride.

Later, I was in a celebratory mood. I had a room with a view in the Hyatt Hotel on Sunset. Hollywood was at my feet. Life was beautiful. I felt on top of the world.

A news clipping from Ty's time on *Star Search*.

HE'S A STAR — Ty Herndon of Decatur will compete in the semi-finals of the syndicated "Star Search" and vie for a $100,000 grand prize and the title of "Best New Star of 1984" this weekend and Feb. 24. Also in the competition are the Decatur brother and sister dance team of Mark and Laura Sellers. "Star Search" will air next year and for those interested in competing may send a tape and resume to the show at Box STAR, 8033 Sunset Blvd., Hollywood, CA 90069.

Ty on *Star Search*.

CHAPTER 8

RAPE

I'VE CHARACTERIZED THIS incident in many ways. I've called it unforeseen or unfortunate. I've minimized it. For years, I've tried to wipe it from my memory, to pretend it didn't happen. Or that it did, but it wasn't a big deal.

Yet trauma can't be dismissed. Trauma is a monster that, until you deal with it, only becomes more monstrous. Trauma corrodes your sanity. It took years for me to understand the depths and damage of the corrosion. Even now this is a chapter in my life I don't want to document. But it happened.

It began simply. Someone who worked for *Star Search* invited me to dinner at the hotel where I was staying. He was a man in his forties. I was twenty-one. He congratulated and flattered me effusively. He was sophisticated and smart. He said he could help me. He ordered sushi—a first for me. For dessert we had crème brûlée, another first. After a couple of glasses of wine, we decided to keep the conversation going up in my room. I saw him as someone who wanted to both befriend and mentor me.

He mixed a drink of vodka and cranberry juice. It tasted sweet but strange. I was only a very occasional drinker, so my frame of reference was limited. Only later did I realize that he had dropped in a pill that made me loopy and loose. When he poured some white powder out on the desk and arranged the substance in neat lines, I was reluctant. I had enough coherence to ask what it was.

"Just something to make you feel better," he said.

"Is it coke?" I asked. I'd never done any drug.

"No, no," he insisted. "Just a little speed. You'll love it."

This was my introduction to crystal meth, the drug that switched up my brain and rearranged the course of my life.

On that night, though, I wasn't thinking of my future. I wasn't thinking at all. The wine and vodka and the pill, the unsettling energy engendered by the meth—it all conspired to put me in a state of confusion.

About one thing, though, I'm not confused: what happened next happened without my permission. I think about why I didn't say no. Why I so readily submitted. Surely it was the drug that made me passive, but was it also my insane need to please everyone? Did it have to do with my undiagnosed mental condition, a budding sexual addiction that would play out many years later? Was it the way in which my brain so frequently misfired? Or was this just how the business worked?

I can't say. All I know is that this *Star Search* staffer who was promoting my talent, violated my trust and my body. The drugs gave me no opportunity to say no. The pain was excruciating. My cries were ignored. I was too weak to fight back. When it was over, he left without a word. My body collapsed; my mind went numb.

It was soon dawn and he was finally gone. I wanted to believe that it was all a bad dream. But the pain in my body said otherwise.

I walked onto the balcony outside my room and looked down fourteen floors onto a deserted Sunset Boulevard. The world was still there. The world didn't know what had happened to me. The world didn't care. Night had turned to day. A billboard displayed Sylvester Stallone as Rambo in *First Blood*. I felt drained of all living energy. I wanted to disappear. I was enveloped by humiliation and self-loathing. It was my fault. I had agreed to dinner. I had let him into my room. I must have let him know that I wanted sex. I had betrayed June. Betrayed God. I wanted to die.

I put my right foot over the balcony. As I began to lift my left foot, I felt a strong hand on my shoulder and heard someone shout, "No!" I turned and saw a tiny Latina woman. She was wearing the white uniform of a hotel employee. Her eyes were wide with a mixture of alarm and decisiveness. She gripped me with both hands and would not let go. She kept shaking her head and repeating, "No, no, no." She led me back into the room. I didn't resist. Her intervention was no accident. Why was she there to clean the room at such an early hour? As I sat on the bed and wept, she brought me tissues. She touched my cheek and spoke to me with her eyes. Her eyes said, "Stay. Live." Then she left.

I slept for many hours. When I awoke, showered, and dressed, I went looking for the lady who had saved me. But the manager said that no one had been cleaning rooms at 6:00 a.m. Even today, I have no explanation. All I know is that this unnamed angel kept me from jumping.

I was alive, but I had no tools to deal with what had happened. The word "trauma" was not part of my vocabulary then. My view of homosexuality had always been essentially negative, but now homosexuality was tied to rape. Now my identity was fully broken in two.

One side represented talent and love and June; the other homosexuality and horror and guilt and shame.

That afternoon I showed up at the studio where they were taping another episode on which I was to appear. Minutes after I arrived, I saw my assailant. He was dressed in designer jeans and a camel-colored cashmere sport jacket. He looked like a *GQ* model. He looked right through me. Not even a nod. I felt sick to my stomach.

I can always sing—except this time I couldn't. Not well. My pitch was off and my phrasing uneven. I couldn't even remember the lyrics. All I know is that I butchered it. Justifiably, the judges gave me a dismal grade. This was a major humiliation in an area where I'd never been humiliated. I went back to Nashville in a state of extreme mortification. I had not only performed dismally but I was also living with the secret of this violent assault. When family and friends asked how I did on the second show—which had yet to air—I mumbled something like "Well, not as good as the first show."

I was afforded some grace when Sam Riddle, the big shot who owned *Star Search*, intervened. He instructed his musical director to fly to Nashville and have me dub over my poor vocal. That meant that when the show aired, my singing sounded great. That didn't explain, however, why the judges gave me a low score. The at-home audience didn't know that my original vocal was subpar. And I didn't explain why. I was too ashamed. Like untold zillions of victims of sexual assault, I had somehow twisted the story inside my mind to where the fault was mine. I wanted to tell someone, but who? As months went by, I agonized about whether I should tell Sam Riddle himself. After all, he had been kind to me. He recognized my talent. He allowed me to save face and redo the bad vocals. He seemed like a fair and decent guy. Wouldn't he want to know what one of his execs had done to me? Shouldn't I tell him what had happened to prevent it from happening to someone else?

If I were to tell Mr. Riddle, how would I do it? I was no longer a contestant on the show. Would I call him? Would he even take my call? Or, if he did, was this something to even talk about on the phone? Didn't it demand an in-person meeting? Was I ready to spend the money on a trip to LA just to cry my heart out to a man I barely knew?

I wrestled with these questions for months. For all that time, I was broken. I kept all this to myself. I didn't discuss it with my mother or sister or any of my friends. The pain festered inside.

But then my mood suddenly transformed when the phone rang. It was Mr. Riddle! He was calling to say that because my initial appearance had scored so high, I was in the semifinals. I'd be going to LA, on his dime, with a shot of getting to the finals.

That changed everything. Because Mr. Riddle had expressed such respect for my talent, I took that as the sign I needed that he would be open to hearing what had happened to me. But first, two more *Star Search* appearances. My Opryland family was super excited that I was back on the show.

Before I knew it, I was heading to Hollywood. I wanted this to be the most special moment of my life. In some ways, it was. Yet I could hardly forget that I was returning to the scene of the crime. It didn't help that the show booked us at the same Hyatt. That first night I couldn't sleep.

The day of the semifinals, my friend Sam Harris and I were chatting. Sam had performed spectacularly throughout the season and was the overwhelming favorite to win it all.

"How are you feeling, buddy?" I asked him.

"Great, until I saw you," he said with a smile. "You're the only one I'm worried about."

"Thanks for the compliment, but I don't think you need to worry."

I meant it. I was a long shot even to make the finals. And yet the long shot came in. Singing "The Wind Beneath My Wings," I gave it all I had, and miraculously won my way into the finals.

Mom and Dad were so excited that they decided to fly out to LA so they could sit in the studio audience and cheer me on. This was a big deal. Their first plane ride. And the first time Dad had ever shown me this kind of support. I was thrilled.

During dinner the night before the show, Dad played down his excitement, but I could feel his pride. I kept talking about how Sam Harris was a shoo-in, but Dad wouldn't hear of it.

"Been listening to you sing, son, ever since you were a little boy," he said, "and I know you're the best. That's all there is to it."

Ty and Mama Peggy at *Star Search* in 1982.

The crybaby in me came out at that table. I couldn't stop the tears. Dad had never talked this way before.

Next afternoon, showtime. *Here we go. Let's do this thing, Ty. Let's nail it.*

I felt like I did. With huge emotion, I sang Kenny Rogers's "Love the World Away" from *Urban Cowboy*. Mom and Dad jumped to their feet, hooting and hollering. The judges liked what they heard, but there was no beating Sam. This was Sam's season. He easily took first place with his scintillating version of "Somewhere Over the Rainbow." In the aftermath, he was offered a Motown recording contract. Other contestants got major-label deals as well. I didn't. That left me feeling disappointed, frustrated, and angry. But I held the anger in. Like at so many other times in my life, I put up a façade. I simply put my best foot forward. I acted like, *Oh well, at least I made a good showing.*

During the post-taping party, there were cheers all around. I was feeling grateful for making the finals. I was also amazed when Dad actually hugged me tight and said for the first time ever, "Son, I'm proud of you." That's a moment in time that lives with me to this day.

I made a point to introduce my folks to Mr. Riddle. I hoped he would sing my praises to them, and he did. That made me postpone my plan to have a come-to-Jesus talk with him. I was doing pretty good until I saw the rapist approaching us. I froze. I wanted to run but there wasn't time. He had this big shit-eating grin on his face. Why was he smiling? Why in hell was he even coming near me? Casually, he introduced himself to my parents, as if nothing had happened. Watching my father shake this man's hand was excruciating. Everything in me wanted to tell Dad what this man had done. I wanted to scream it. At the same time, I fantasized what Dad would do to this man had he known the truth: He'd bash the fucker's brains out.

That did it. I decided to tell Mr. Riddle what had been boiling up inside me for months.

Later that day I went to the production office. I asked whether the boss was in. I hoped he was but also hoped he wasn't.

He was in.

Big gulp.

I walked into his office. He looked up and said, "Hey, Ty, great show. What gives?"

Short in stature and plainspoken, Sam Riddle had a bit of Dick Clark's looks but none of Dick's charm. He was a straight-ahead businessman.

"Oh, I just wanted to thank you for being so nice to my folks." Ready to turn around and fly home to Nashville. I didn't think I could handle this confrontation. But I also couldn't handle staying silent. I'd spent a hundred hours thinking about what had happened. I had to say something. And I did. I spit it all out. I told Sam Riddle how I'd been drugged and raped by his employee. I expected him to be enraged.

"Look, Ty," he said, "things can get out of hand. But this is something you've got to forget. If you tell this story, it will end your career. Besides, this is just one show that I produce. I'm planning other talent shows where I can use you. You're a good-looking kid with a great voice. Don't fuck up your future."

I was too stunned to reply. I didn't have the strength to argue. I didn't have the presence to say, "I can call the police. I can go public. I can cause a scandal."

In the end, I did nothing. I just got up to leave. I didn't even refuse when he offered his hand for me to shake.

I followed Sam Riddle's instructions. I kept quiet and flew back to Nashville where I couldn't be myself. For days I suffered in silence. I finally called Carl Peoples, the first and only person I told for years.

Carl is a brother from another mother. He knew what to say.

"You've been violated in the worst possible way, Ty. Try not to blame yourself. You need help. Please get some counseling."

I didn't argue with Carl. I've never argued with him. But the idea of therapy didn't seem plausible. I could talk to Carl about what had happened, but I couldn't imagine talking to a stranger.

Despite the real-life nightmare that I suffered in that hotel room, my desire for stardom hadn't diminished. I put my career before my mental health. I repressed like I had never repressed before. True to his word, Sam Riddle had me flying back and forth to LA to perform on his other shows. The Tennessee River Boys did fine without me. They morphed into Diamond Rio and enjoyed massive hits.

Meanwhile, I was still engaged to June.

"You shouldn't be," my mother told me.

"Why?"

"You know why. That's not who you are."

As best I can recall, this was the first time Mom openly implied that I was gay. Her acknowledgment of my true nature touched me and drew me even closer to her. No one understood me like she did. And yet— and here's the crazy part—I still stayed engaged to June. I was still determined to carry out my All-American plan of having a wife and kids.

Our engagement lasted a while longer. Finally, though, I liked June too much to keep up the façade. One Sunday after church we took a long walk. She could sense that my heart was heavy.

"Go ahead and say what you have to say, Ty," she urged. "If you want to break up with me, then just say so."

I was sweating profusely. I desperately did not want to hurt June. But I also did not want to tell the truth. Yet at this point the guilt was too much to bear. I finally found the courage to admit that I was attracted to both men and women and that I had not been monogamous. June wasn't surprised. She had surmised as much. End of engagement. Beginning of . . . what?

I wasn't sure. But I *was* sure that if I told the world I was gay, the world of country music would reject me out of hand. In that world, where I so badly wanted to be a star, I would never make it.

Ty (center) and the Tennessee River Boys.

CHAPTER 9

LIFE AND DEATH

THOUGH MY PARENTS had traveled together to Hollywood to see me on *Star Search*, their marriage was unraveling. The most tolerant and patient of women, Mom was tired of Dad's jealousy, dominance, and drinking. Mom lived in the same house with Dad, but for how much longer I didn't know. Miss Peggy was unhappy, and because Miss Peggy was—and is—my heart, I was unhappy as well.

I managed to maintain a semblance of sanity by entertaining on cruise ships. Those gigs were great escapes. The shows were extravagant, the audiences appreciative, and the food great. I was a featured attraction. I still hadn't secured a record deal, but thanks to my TV appearances, I was making a living.

Cruises kept me focused on my singing. Not to mention sex. I didn't have to cruise on the cruise ship. The large troupe included gay guys who, like me, felt a certain freedom being in the middle of the Caribbean. It was a continuation of the hit-and-split promiscuity that I'd discovered at Opryland. Now I see it as more addictive behavior; then I saw it as harmless escape. I could be my true self because I wasn't trying to make it in showbiz in any traditional way. I was just getting paid to sing.

For months I sailed those seas, giving and getting pleasure. Onstage, my repertoire widened. For the first time, I got into pop and sang songs by Deniece Williams and the Pointer Sisters.

The cruise stopped in Aruba, where I went into a souvenir shop and selected a postcard showing a pink-and-purple sunrise. I felt moved to write to my father, something I'd never done.

"Thanks for being in my corner, Dad," I wrote. "I love you."

A week later a telegram arrived. My first thought was that Sam Riddle was calling me to Hollywood for another television show. Instead, the message was from Mom: "Your father's had a stroke. Come home quick as you can."

I made it to Decatur in less than two days, but even that was too late. By the time I arrived, he was gone. Wesley Boyd Herndon, dead of a massive stroke at age forty-five. It was hard to accept. The shock was seismic. No one could believe it. I cried when Mom said that the last thing he'd read was my postcard. I couldn't stop thinking of that precious moment when, after my *Star Search* loss, he hugged me and expressed approval.

At the graveside service, I remembered when he and Mom had come to Nashville to see a new apartment I'd rented. I was proud of a waterbed I had put together. He walked into the bedroom and carefully inspected the bed. I desperately wanted his admiration then too, and held my breath until he finally said, "Well done."

I heard those words in my head as his casket was lowered into the ground.

Mom never let go of my hand. She would never marry again. As a result of Dad's unexpected death, Mom and I became even closer.

Fatherless, I ventured forward. I didn't know where I was going, but I was in a hurry to get there.

Ty and Mama Peggy on his very first Country Cruise booking in 2002.

CHAPTER 10

MEET MISS NORTH CAROLINA

DONNA LEIGH WILSON was a great beauty, a statuesque blonde, a polished professional who began winning pageants as a young girl growing up in North Carolina. She quickly became queen of the state.

I met Donna through Leigh Brannon, one of my best friends, who produced local pageants and hired me to sing at many of them. We lovingly called Leigh "Lizard" because of how she slithered into and out of rooms.

I loved playing pageants and was in great form when I came face-to-face with Donna. It happened while I was singing Julio Iglesias's "To All the Girls I've Loved Before" at a competition in Raleigh-Durham. My performance had me singing up close and personal to each contestant for several seconds. When I came to Donna, I lingered a bit longer. After she won, I congratulated her on her victory, and she, in turn, congratulated me on my performance. Both Southerners, both extroverts, we felt an immediate connection. Beyond her perky personality, I could feel her toughness. Donna was a tough broad, and a funny one to boot. We were kindred souls.

When I asked her out, she picked the spot.

"Let's go to a gay bar," she suggested.

That took me aback. "Why a gay bar?" I had to know.

"Because I want to get smashed," she said. "Beauty queens aren't supposed to get smashed. But when I get smashed at a gay bar and someone recognizes me, they won't go blabbing because they won't want to admit where they saw me."

I laughed uneasily. Did she know my secret? Did she care?

When we got smashed and started dancing, all my worries vanished. The fast dancing was fun and the slow dancing fed my romantic side. Only a few dates later we were frolicking in bed. It was the hottest female frolicking I'd ever known. It was more than Donna's phenomenal body. It was her likability. Her sass. Her guts.

Donna was a blast. The blast was big enough to make me believe—once again—that I could live the life of a straight man. Donna had no reason to believe I wasn't straight. The words "I love you" fell naturally from our lips. Plus, I felt proud. I had won the heart of a genuine beauty queen!

Our relationship was easy-breezy. I had my professional agenda, and Donna had hers. She was winning beauty contests, including the prestigious Miss North Carolina pageant, while I was playing cruises and appearing on a few Sam Riddle TV shows like *You Write the Songs* and the special *America's Top Model*.

Although we never lived together, Donna and I considered ourselves a couple. The only painful incident occurred at a beauty contest in South Carolina. I sang, and Donna won first place. She was on her way to another pageant in Georgia. I was due to leave the next morning. Late that night I got into the hotel elevator to go to my room. I was wearing a pink sequined jacket with an undeniable Liberace vibe. Three rednecks got on the elevator with me and picked up that vibe. They started calling me a faggot.

"I'm straight," I argued.

They didn't buy it. Instead, they beat the shit out of me. They gave me a black eye and nearly busted my nose. When I told Donna, she was incensed. But I would soon learn that the "I'm straight" plea rang hollow to people other than homophobic rednecks.

Donna kept an apartment in Manhattan, where she had launched a successful modeling and acting career. Her roommate was Danny, a gay man eleven years our senior. She described me to Danny as the man of her dreams. All this was well and good until I came to New York for a weekend visit.

"Sit down, Ty," she said. "I have something to tell you."

I sat.

"I'm seeing someone."

I was neither surprised nor angry. We had never pledged monogamy. Of course other men would pursue Donna. Donna was a doll. It was her next statement, though, that hit me like a punch in the gut.

"Besides, Ty, you're gay."

"I am?"

"Of course you are, sweetheart. We've both known that but haven't wanted to say it."

Donna was right. I guess we had always shared an unspoken understanding. And now that it was out in the open, I felt relief. I felt even more love for Donna!

"Look, Ty," she said. "Since you're here, why don't you spend the week with my roommate Danny? He's adorable. You're adorable. You'll have fun together."

And we did. The switch was seamless. Rather than stay in Donna's bedroom, I shacked up with Danny, a sophisticated gent who took me to New York's fabulous gay bars.

As improbable as it sounds, the transition was silky smooth. Even though Donna and I might not have been *in* love, we certainly did love each other. She presented Danny as a gift that I accepted with enormous pleasure.

Donna's acting career flourished. In 1990, she met director Tony Scott (of *Top Gun* fame) during the making of *Days of Thunder*. They married four years later and had two beautiful twin boys. We all remained family.

Lizard was pleased to see that my relationship with Donna survived. Lizard was one of a kind, a short, fetching blonde with smoldering green eyes. She was a go-getter, a whip-smart organizer who later founded the first Ty Herndon fan club. She was crucial to my ever-changing, challenging career.

Ty learning choreography for the pageant at which he met future Miss North Carolina Donna Wilson.

CHAPTER 11

MEET THE COWBOY

WES MEYERS, MY buddy from Opryland, was living in Fort Worth, Texas, where he leased apartments. He had a boyfriend and a happy home life. Unlike me, Wes wasn't driven to make his mark in music. But he knew I was.

In the mid-eighties, he called to say, "Tyrone, get your ass down to Texas. You'll make a ton of money playing the clubs here."

I followed his advice and found weekend work in Dallas. It didn't take long before I became a local favorite and headlined at the Rodeo Exchange—the Carnegie Hall of honky-tonks—where I met and befriended Troy Aikman, the heroic quarterback of the Dallas Cowboys and a die-hard country music fan.

It was the start of a new decade—the nineties—and I was singing jingles and making demos for other artists. My colleagues from *Star Search*—top-notch artists like Sam Harris and Sawyer Brown—had the backing of powerful record companies. Justifiably, they had become stars. The fact that stardom had eluded me was an ongoing source of frustration. Further frustration came from my inability to make a living as a recording artist.

At one point it looked like my big break was at hand. A record company was on the verge of offering me a deal. The CEO, though, nixed it when he met me in person. His rejection stung: "Son," he said, "you're too pretty for country music. Get on your little red tractor and head back to Alabama." I wanted to snap back "Fuck you," but held my tongue. Instead of "too pretty," I got the idea that he wanted to say "too gay." It was another time when I figured discretion was the better part of valor. But this valor thing was wearing me out.

My permanent home was a Nashville condo that I shared with my mom, who was working at JCPenney, and my sister. I was basically commuting to Texas on the weekends, where I'd put together a band called Ty Herndon and Ryde the West. We used "Ryde" because we were going from gig to gig in a Ryder truck. We thought the Ryder folks would understand. Wrong. When Ryder learned about us, they threatened to sue. Because we had no money for lawyers, we dropped the *Y* and rechristened ourselves Ride the West.

Rodeo Exchange was crowded the night the Cowboy first appeared, but I spotted him right away. He was drop-dead Robert Redford handsome. His black cowboy hat and alligator boots added to his swag. Masculine to a fault, he couldn't have acted any straighter.

During my break, I sent a round of beers over to his table and dropped by to meet him. The Cowboy and I locked eyes. Shaking his hand, I felt an electrical current run up my arm. During my next set, I tried not to look in his direction but failed.

A few nights later he returned. We said hello again, but that was all. On the third night he showed up, we went to a quiet corner table and started talking.

"Glad to see you back here," I said.

"Glad to be back."

"I'm guessing you like the music."

"I'm coming back for more than the music."

"So why *are* you coming back?" I asked, even though I damn well knew the answer.

"I'd like to hang out after your last set."

I cut my last set short. The hangout turned out to be in his fancy office only a fifteen minutes' drive away. We made love on his office couch.

The Cowboy was too good to be true.

For the next several weeks, I came to believe that he was, in fact, not true at all. That's because after our initial hookup he stopped coming to the club. I looked for him every night. When he missed one night, I thought, *Okay, he's busy. No big deal.* After two nights, I got nervous. After a whole week, I was a wreck. And then after two weeks, I felt my heart crack in half. I'd been duped. Whatever I'd felt was just lust. What we'd had was another cheap one-night affair.

And then, just when I was at my lowest, I came home to find a FedEx letter waiting for me. It was from the Cowboy. My heart dropped to the floor. I was sure he was saying goodbye before we had even said hello. But no—he was saying that he'd been out of touch because of something he had to take care of before seeing me again: He had to deal with his wife. His wife! Who knew that he was married? No matter; he told his wife that he wanted a divorce. He told her that he had met someone else. Their marriage was never going to work. She agreed. A divorce was forthcoming. Now he felt free to see me. Did I want to see him?

Did I!

That very night he showed up. From then on, we were inseparable.

Our favorite spot became the Round-Up Saloon, a gay country-western dance hall where, just as I had been a roller-skating king as a kid, I was now king of the two-step. I loved two-stepping and line dancing. And especially loved doing it with my new man.

A month after we met, he divorced his wife. A few weeks later, we started living together in the stately five-bedroom home that had belonged to his aunt. The house was situated in Highland Park, the most prestigious old-guard neighborhood in Dallas. On top of that, he bought me a brand-new Mercedes—and a matching one for himself.

The Cowboy was my first rescue relationship. Because my music career wasn't paying the bills, he rescued me from financial insecurity. He also rescued me from the world of promiscuity. He wanted us to be monogamous. I wanted that as well. The Cowboy was adamant about remaining closeted. He didn't want to risk losing his prominence in the community. That was fine with me. Everything about the Cowboy was fine with me.

Meanwhile, Wes Meyers pointed me in a new direction. He said I'd be good at leasing apartments. As a day job, I could make seven hundred dollars a week. So, Wes hooked me up with a firm in Irving, a burb just outside Dallas. I landed the job not because of my qualifications but because of how I answered the manager's question.

"Can I drive your Benz at lunch each day?" she asked.

"Sure," I said.

Done deal.

Life became brighter when Mom moved to Dallas, where JCPenney offered her a better job. Dallas was also the home of her sister Greta. Mom and Aunt Greta were about the only two outsiders who knew the truth about me and the Cowboy. Turned out that they were also crazy about him and became regular visitors at our Highland Park home.

It was in Mom's presence that the Cowboy presented me with a pair of seven-hundred-dollar boots. Not long after, he bought Mom a gorgeous emerald ring. We all became family. The Cowboy came to love Wes Meyers as a brother and Leigh "Lizard" Brannon as a sister. In the meantime, Lizard was living in North Carolina. She called and said she was in an unhappy marriage, and would I come get her?

I did.

CHAPTER 12

MEET THE DRAG QUEEN

I'LL CALL HER Miss G. Miss G was something else. A heavyset Black man who, in drag, became a regal diva. Miss G spoke the Queen's English and treated me like kin. Miss G was both my sister and my drug dealer.

Crystal meth was reintroduced to me long after I'd met the Cowboy, who had nothing to do with it. He was a straight shooter who hated drugs. His only stimulant was sex with me. Without the Cowboy knowing, I built up an addiction to the crystal meth that was everywhere in the club scene back then. In fact, it was the club owners who, seeing I was tired between my fourth and fifth shows, first offered me a bump. I didn't think twice about it. It was just an energy boost. No big deal.

Though meth was the same drug I'd taken before I was raped, I had disassociated from that event. In fact, taking the drug helped erase that memory; meth sped me up and fast-forwarded me to another place. I liked what it did to my brain. My speedy brain liked getting even speedier. The speed fueled another fast-growing addiction: porn.

Nothing I liked more than getting high and running over to the gay bookstore on Greenville Avenue to check out the magazines and rent VHS tapes. Before long, I felt like I was personal friends with every gay porn star.

On one humid Dallas night, I got to the bookstore a half hour before they were closing, and other than the man at the cash register, no one was there except Miss G, adorned in a red hoop dress. She looked like the belle of the ball.

"You don't need porn," she said to me. "You need food."

She took me to her lavishly decorated apartment near White Rock Lake. The wallpaper was glossy gold and the shag carpet lily white. She changed into a robe of royal blue and sat me at her kitchen table as she cooked me pork chops and fried potatoes. I'd never tasted anything so good. We never had sex. I wasn't her type and she wasn't mine, but we understood each other.

"Ty," she said, "you're the only person I know who can get high on this shit and still eat a whole plate of pork chops."

She warned me about cruising; she chastised me for getting dope from a club owner notorious for using inferior product. If I wanted to get high, she had the goods, including crystal meth. She gave me a sample that had me soaring.

"You take care, baby," Miss G said just before I left. "But just remember this. I sell top-quality product and make no apologies. But for folks I like—folks like you—I always tack on a warning: The meth will make you feel good, but the meth can also fuck you up to where the good feeling ain't worth it. You hear me, sugar?"

"I hear you, but I'm not worried," I said. "I can handle it."

I kissed Miss G on the cheek and was back the next night. I wanted more meth, but I also wanted her company.

"A good-looking guy like you has to be careful," she said. "You can break a lot of hearts."

I didn't want to break the Cowboy's heart—and was somehow able to keep him from knowing about my high life. We both worked strange hours, and besides, he trusted me. His trust enabled me to go beyond the closeted life I was living with two other secrets: I was getting high on meth while masturbating to porn.

I could easily hide my drug high because of my naturally bubbly personality. I was blessed with the gift of gab. I loved meeting new people. I loved mingling with my fans, the more the merrier. One such fan turned out to be a captain of industry who couldn't understand why I wasn't a big star.

Enter Bill Perry, wealthy owner of a textile firm. Bill had heard me in the clubs and was sure he could persuade a Texas record label to give me a deal. He got me to quit my apartment leasing job and put me on his payroll at $650 a week. I had no responsibilities other than to form a new band. Bill paid for everything. He knew nothing about my drug use, but he did know I was gay.

"You can't be gay and get a deal," he said. "You need to get a wife."

This was a big moment. I paused for a few seconds before responding. In those few seconds, I reconsidered my situation. I thought of the country music culture. I knew that culture well. And I knew that was a culture where gay men had no place. No culture in this country was more macho. I further knew that was the culture in which I wanted to succeed. If success meant denying my own nature, well, I was willing.

Yes, sir, I will find a wife.

At the apartment leasing firm, the woman who sat at the desk next to mine was KaSondra Hays. We'd become fast friends. She had a fabulous figure and a fondness for gay men. While I didn't come out to her, she always knew. That's why, when I asked her a surprising question, she didn't bat an eye.

"Will you marry me?" was the question.

"Why, of course," she said.

KaSondra happened to be going through a tough breakup of her own, so my proposal came at the right time.

I had no hesitation, but when I told Mom the plan, she raised her eyebrow.

"Tyrone," she said, "why do you have to go through another charade?"

"It's a business decision," I said.

"I don't buy that, son."

"The industry just won't accept me as gay."

"Your father would have."

"What makes you say that?"

"Back in Decatur, his best friend was gay."

"Gary was gay?"

"And your dad couldn't have cared less."

I remember Gary as a good-looking guy. I'd assumed he was straight. I'd assumed all the guys in Dad's circle were straight. Obviously, there was a side to Dad that I didn't know. Did he know that I was gay and, without saying so, had he accepted me as such? Was he more open-minded than I could ever have imagined? All my life I had assumed that my father hated having a gay son. Now I was confused and had to reassess. I desperately wanted to bring back my father so I could better understand him. Now I could only talk to him in my dreams. I could only guess the way he really felt about me and my sexual nature.

Anyway, the news that Gary was gay shocked the hell out of me. But I had no reason to doubt Mom. She had good judgment.

I did not. I was sure marrying KaSondra was the way to take my career to the next level. So, after securing the approval of the Cowboy, who favored anything that kept us in the closet, I went ahead. KaSondra and I went to the courthouse and tied the knot.

You'd think that with my life changing so radically—after all, marriage is a big deal—I'd slow down for a minute or two to reflect. Well, think again. Crystal meth had me in manic mode.

The day after our wedding, I had a gig in Oklahoma. Before KaSondra and I took off, I wrote up a big banner—"JUST MARRIED!"—and plastered it on the bumper of my car. I put the sign there at the request of Bill Perry, who wanted to publicize the event. And although the Cowboy gave the marriage his blessing, KaSondra wondered whether the Cowboy was worried that she would convert me. I didn't think so. It was simply that the super-conservative Cowboy was uncomfortable around the free-spirited KaSondra. He was afraid that she'd say the wrong thing at the wrong time. He didn't trust her impulsivity.

Later KaSondra did admit that she had fantasized about consummating our marriage. But she knew me well enough to understand that my physical desire was completely directed toward the Cowboy. In KaSondra's circle, only her mother knew that the marriage was a front. Fortunately, her mom, like my mom, made no judgments.

There was the night KaSondra and her mother came to see me perform.

While I was on stage singing, one of my female fans said to KaSondra, "I'm gonna have sex with your husband tonight."

"Honey," said my wife, "if you can get him, you can have him."

KaSondra's mom fell out laughing.

We all agreed that KaSondra would be happiest living in the guest quarters next to our house in Highland Park. But that lasted only a week.

"I feel like a third wheel here," she said. "I'd better find a place of my own."

"Probably a good idea," I agreed.

The Cowboy fixed her up in a nice apartment in Irving close to the leasing office.

After six months, when Bill Perry failed to get me a record deal, KaSondra and I decided to divorce. Why shouldn't KaSondra have the chance to meet someone interested in a real marriage? In fact, she eventually did find a good man and get married.

Years later, someone asked KaSondra why she would ever marry me.

"Because I loved him," she said.

I felt the same. I had big love for KaSondra.

Playing the clubs, I was always super-charming with the ladies, but sometimes the cowboys didn't like that. Once at a meet-and-greet with fans, a young woman sat on my lap and asked for a photo. Her boyfriend became instantly jealous and lashed out at me with, "You're a little too pretty for country music anyway. You're probably a homo."

I couldn't stand for that, of course. So, I shot back, "Fuck you—in your dreams," and a scuffle ensued. The fight ended when he stabbed me with a pen. Can you imagine? And the kicker? She still wanted her photo with me, and I still have the scar to this day.

Meanwhile, career-wise, I was back to square one. For all her valiant efforts, Lizard, now my manager, couldn't get me a deal either. My sister, Alicia, and her husband, Donny Thompson, a drummer and producer, also tried. They found two other extremely talented producers—Michael Knox and Lauren Pendergrast—who helped me make a series of demos. Sony/Epic Nashville showed some interest but ultimately passed. That's why I was reluctant when a Nashville friend told me that I should knock on Sony's door again.

"What's the point?" I asked.

"Warner Brothers passed on Randy Travis ten times before they signed him," said my pal. "Trust me. Make a call, and I'll bet the bigwigs will see you. You're better known than you realize."

Even those words of encouragement weren't enough to get me to reapproach Sony/Epic. It took a sequence of unexpected events to make that happen.

In 1993, at age thirty-one, I was named Texas Entertainer of the Year, the first non-Texan to win the award. At the ceremony in Austin, Peter Svenson, an independent promotor, heard me and alerted his friend Margie Hunt, a Sony/Epic exec, who came to Dallas to see me perform at the Country Connection. Margie was excited enough to make a second trip, this time with Doug Johnson, Sony/Epic VP, who liked what he heard and invited me to Nashville to perform for their boss, label president Allen Butler.

A week later, I walked into the Epic Nashville conference room. Doug and Margie were seated at one end of the table. Seated alone at the far end was Allen Butler. The room was hot and stuffy. My mouth was dry. My stomach was filled with butterflies. Although I knew Doug and Margie were on my side, Butler gave no sign of approval. In fact, he sat there at the head of the table with his arms crossed over his chest, looking skeptical.

"Where's your guitar?" asked Butler.

"I don't play guitar," I admitted. "I just use it as a prop."

"Okay, but where's your hat?"

I wasn't wearing a cowboy hat that day. The question made me even more nervous. Sweat ran down my back.

"Am I here to talk about props or to talk about music?" I asked.

"Music," said Butler. "Forget the hat and guitar. I wanna hear you sing. But how are you gonna do that without music?"

"I grew up Pentecostal," I said. That meant I could sing fully a cappella.

"Fair enough," said Butler. "Let's hear you."

Unaccompanied, I sang a version of "How Great Thou Art," complete with key changes.

"Great," said Johnson, "but can you sing something country?"

"I'm going to sing a song I sang at the Grand Ole Opry, where I was introduced by Roy Acuff."

I broke into Jack Greene's "There Goes My Everything." I sang the shit out of it.

Yet when I hit the last note, there was silence. I didn't know what to think or do. No one said a word. So, I turned around and walked out to my truck. I thought I'd nailed the audition, but I guessed I was wrong. Then I heard Margie's voice.

"Hey, Ty, where you going?" she yelled.

"Going to have some lunch."

Actually, meth was gonna be my lunch.

"Come back in. We're offering you a deal!"

When I returned to the conference room, the vibe was totally different. Smiles, handshakes, and hugs all around. Allen Butler was suddenly my best friend. He wanted to hear how I came up. I spoke about singing on Grandma Myrtle's radio show when I was four.

"That's a perfect backstory for a country singer. The press will eat it up," said Butler.

He was right. My signing made *Entertainment Tonight*, where I got to talk about my childhood in rural Alabama. A television crew went to Butler to interview my family. Everyone suddenly started losing their Southern accents. It reminded me of the episode of *The Andy Griffith Show* when Earl Scruggs visits and Mayberry gets to putting on airs. "Hey, folks," I told my people, "talk the way you always talk. The more genuine you are, the better."

I was one to talk.

At my next label meeting, Butler introduced me to Joe Diffie, a hugely successful Epic country artist whose *Honky Tonk Attitude* had gone platinum, with three top ten singles.

"Welcome aboard, Ty," said Diffie. "I'm a big fan. Word is, Epic is betting big on you."

"Hell, yes," said Butler. "We're planning the biggest rollout since Patty Loveless. Ty, the money train's about to drive right up your ass."

The metaphor seemed a little strange to me. Was Butler referring

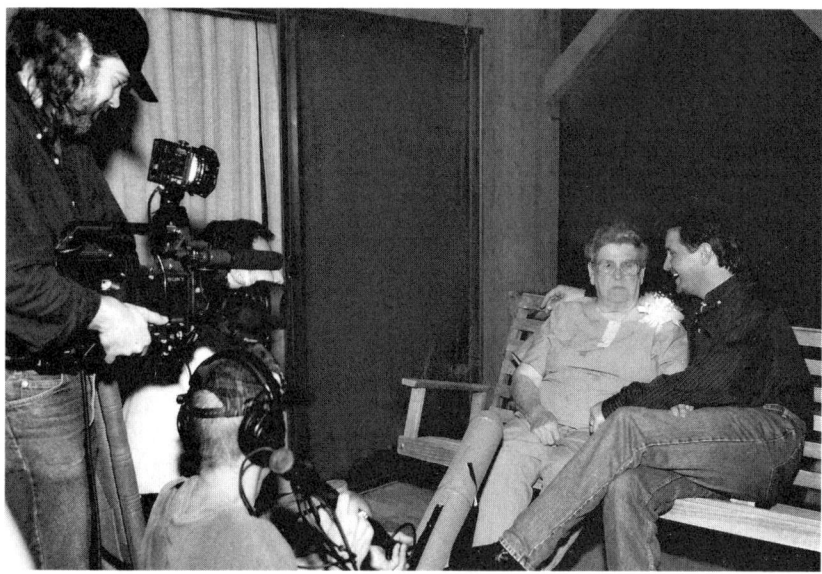

In 1995, Sony/Epic traveled to Butler, Alabama, to chronicle Ty's life back home. This is Ty on the front porch swing with Grandma Myrtle.

to my secret sex life? Surely that was just my paranoia. The reality was that I had a record deal with Sony/Epic Nashville. I had a beautiful relationship with the Cowboy. I had a few secrets, but I had things under control.

What more did I need?

CHAPTER 13

"YOU NEED TO MEET CHER"

THAT'S WHAT THE Sony team told me. I was delighted and a little confused: Why did I need to meet Cher?

"Cher, along with a number of other artists, will be spending a week in Bordeaux, France," said a Sony suit.

"To do what?" I asked.

"Write songs for their new records. It'll serve as a writing course for you."

Great! Sign me up! Fly me first class over the ocean. Put me on a train to Bordeaux! Drive me to the home of Miles Copeland III—the music mogul who managed the Police—and let me gawk!

Who wouldn't gawk at a home that was, in fact, a huge castle? Why wouldn't I be starstruck when, that very first day, I met not only the super-glamorous and super-sweet Cher but also the brilliant singer-songwriters Bruce Roberts, Brenda Russell, Patty Smyth, and Alannah Myles?

At the time, Cher had a hit in Europe—"Save Up All Your Tears," written by Diane Warren and Desmond Child. Bruce Roberts had written a zillion hits, including "No More Tears (Enough Is Enough)" for Barbra Streisand and Donna Summer. Brenda Russell's "Get Here," sung by Oleta Adams, had become an anthem during the recent Gulf War. Alannah Myles had just won a Grammy for Best Female Rock Vocal Performance for "Black Velvet," an homage to Elvis. Patty Smyth had cowritten a smash, "Sometimes Love Just Ain't Enough," that she sang as a duet with Don Henley of the Eagles. Later Patty was my date to the Academy of Country Music Awards. Her boyfriend (later husband), the famously jealous John McEnroe, told her she could do the red carpet with me but nothing more. "But, John," I heard Patty tell him over the phone, "he's gay." No matter; Patty didn't stay. After a polite hug, she departed and headed home.

During this European trip, I was in heady company. I was among artists who, despite their astounding accomplishments, never made me feel less than. They treated me like a colleague. And when they heard me sing, they were delighted. Every night we gathered around the piano with Bruce or Brenda playing their hearts out while we sang anything that came to mind—rock, soul, gospel, country. We also started writing some songs, but few were ever finished. The mandate was to have a good time. For the first five or six days, we just partied.

When the party moved to Paris, Cher learned it was my birthday. She wanted to celebrate with a toast at the Eiffel Tower. So, off we went in a stretch limo the size of a city block. I tried not to play the role of fanboy with Cher, but it wasn't easy. Cher is Cher. Cher is also extremely mothering—in a good way. And, of course, among gay men her iconography is chiseled in Greek marble. Because Cher loves gay men, it's not surprising that I came out to her. Shortly after meeting

Bruce Roberts, for example, I found myself saying, "You're gay, I'm gay, and that's it." In fact, I came out to that whole group, because the whole group made me feel safe.

Atop the Eiffel Tower, with all of Paris at our feet, Cher ordered bottles of Cristal. Ironically, she called me by the same name I called my man in Dallas: "Cowboy."

"You know, Cowboy," said Cher, "you really fascinate me."

"How come?"

"I've never met a masculine cowboy who confesses to being gay."

"I haven't confessed to everyone," I said.

"That's just a matter of time. The world is changing."

She was right, but Nashville wasn't there yet.

Cher and I had a blast that night. It wasn't long before our talk turned into giggles. I got so wasted that the next morning I woke up with a huge hangover. When I gained full consciousness, I realized I was in Cher's suite—and I was wearing nothing but my underwear and a cowboy hat. Bruce Roberts was asleep by the fireplace. Patty was snoozing on the sofa.

I looked up and saw Cher, who was dressed from head to toe in goth black leather.

"Don't even think about it," she said. "Nothing happened. You just never made it back to your room. Now, hurry up and get dressed. Everyone wants to go shopping."

I soon learned that there is no shopping like Paris shopping. The opulent department stores—Printemps, Le Bon Marche. The elegant boutiques—Saint Laurent, Dior. I was dizzy. At Cartier, a necklace adorned with precious black stones caught Cher's eye. When she was told the price, she didn't bat an eye.

"Only ten thousand?" she snapped. "I'll take it."

And with that she slapped down a black Amex, something I had never seen.

Back in Nashville, back in the closet, back in the throes of the Epic machine, the execs asked me what I'd learned in France.

"I want to be as successful as Cher," I said.

"Did you write a hit single?"

"I'm not sure."

"Well, it doesn't matter, because we found a song that's perfect for you. It's a guaranteed smash."

Ty and Cher in Europe, celebrating his thirty-second birthday in 1994.

CHAPTER 14

WHAT MATTERED MOST

IT'S A LONG way from the Avenue des Champs-Élysées to Music Row in Nashville.

Learning that my long-delayed career was about to take off, I had to decide what mattered most: coming out or having a hit record. I knew damn well that the two were mutually exclusive. I went with the hit and kept living the lie—and not just living the lie but doubling down on the lie. The duality of my life became more ingrained.

My old nemesis, the rumor mill, had been working overtime. Ever since Opryland, rumors about my gayness had never stopped. It's hardly surprising that someone at Sony heard those rumors. Because this super-prestigious international label was about to pour money into my debut record, they wanted to squash those rumors.

The head of promotion, Jack Lameier, was a great guy and huge Ty fan. He called me into his office, looked up from his desk, and didn't mince words.

"Son," he said, "you may want to get you a wife."

I didn't miss a beat. Nothing had changed. Homophobic Nashville was as homophobic as ever—and, now more than ever, I knew how to play the game.

If I had to choose big-time success over honesty, give me big-time success.

So here we went again. The Bill Perry scenario revisited. The difference this time was that, despite my short-lived marriage to the wonderful KaSondra, Bill Perry had been unable to land me a deal. Now I already had a deal, and it was just a question of whether I would undermine that deal by coming out or enhance my blooming career by marrying again.

What did my partner, the Cowboy, have to say?

Ever faithful, loving, and understanding, the Cowboy remained deeply closeted. My second marriage would further insulate him, as well as me, from the truth. He liked the idea.

The woman I chose had a big, beautiful personality. Renee and I became buddies when I had a repeat gig at a club in San Angelo, Texas. You had to love Renee. She had a sensational look: beautifully permed blond hair, blue eye shadow, huge breasts, tiny waist, great legs. She was a practicing nurse but also a cowgirl who could drink any cowboy under the table. She ran with an entourage of fun-loving girls who loved hanging with the boys.

When we met, though, Renee was grieving. An adopted child, she had just lost her mom. She was in the process of connecting with her birth mother. Her birth mom was thrilled to be reunited with her daughter. On top of that, I learned that Renee had a sister who was a musician and became part of our ever-growing family.

Renee was stubborn as hell, but the woman had soul. I truly loved her. She was eager to lead a more exciting life. I was a gateway to that life. Like KaSondra before her, Renee liked the idea of becoming Mrs. Herndon.

I brought Renee to Dallas to meet the Cowboy. She liked my man. She liked Dallas. She liked the shimmering two-carat diamond engagement ring that I slipped onto her finger. The ring, like the Cowboy's house, had belonged to his aunt. Renee also liked the lovely Highland Park house I rented for her just a few blocks from us. Her next-door neighbor was newly elected governor George W. Bush. At night, I was careful to park my car in Renee's driveway. I wanted the world to believe that she and I were happily domiciled.

When I told Mom about the new marriage plans, I knew what her reaction would be. The raised eyebrow. The sigh. She never scolded, but neither did she refrain from expressing her true feelings; it pained her to see me still pretending.

Nonetheless, our wedding was a joyful event. I wore a tux with a white lily on my lapel. Renee was gorgeous in a lacy white gown. Fresh flowers everywhere. Our vows were spoken. I kissed the bride.

Ty and Renee at their wedding.

The bride kissed the groom. Everything was photographed and videotaped for full media exposure. Wes Meyers, a beloved witness to the ceremony, came to love Renee as much as I did. The Cowboy was my best man. We booked the honeymoon suite at the Hyatt. Renee was happy to stay there while the Cowboy and I went home.

The marriage was a fabulous fraud that went on for years. I say "fabulous" because Renee was a fabulous character, a big personality, an ultra-glamorous woman. She had a mind of her own. She was fiery and fun and, despite her willingness to go along with the lie, a sincere lady.

Meanwhile, I was a fool. I didn't realize how living a lie would become increasingly toxic. To perpetuate the fraud required dexterous emotional manipulation, the most damaging aspects of which I heaped upon myself. I convinced myself I was getting away with something. With everything.

It's too easy to say that I was careerist, even though I was and still am. I've always wanted as many people as possible to hear me sing. I've always yearned for a mass audience. But my careerism was now all mixed up with my self-loathing. While I relished my love life with the Cowboy, I hated the part of me that had to be hidden. I was certain I had this love-hate conundrum under control, even if keeping it under control meant numbing the pain with crystal meth and porn. Then, and for years to come, there would always be three people in my relationships: my male partner, me, and meth.

Now add a fourth person, a highly spirited woman who had essentially been hired to play the part of my wife. Renee liked the spotlight. Sony hired a team of stylists to work with her. She was naturally pretty, and they only made her prettier. They softened her look and dressed her in elegant satin Ralph Lauren dresses. We rocked red carpets, showing up at every media event in sight. With Renee on my arm, I could face the press with a big smile and feel certain that my image was what the world wanted to see.

This was the Nashville music scene in 1995. I was thirty-three. Fame was around the corner. But before fame came my way, I was aware of what had come before me: In the seventies, Outlaw Country was all the rage. Willie. Waylon. Merle. Outsiders like Johnny Cash became mainstream insiders. Brilliant artists like Kris Kristofferson proved that country songwriters could touch the hearts of every category of music lover.

Some describe the 1980s as country music's "Lost Decade." The insinuation was that country had forgotten its roots and lost its soul. I strongly disagree. Early in the decade, George Strait put out his first album. George Strait is pure country. In 1982, Reba McEntire's "Can't Even Get the Blues No More" beat back the blues and rose to number one. Anne Murray came on strong; Alabama came on strong; and the Outlaws, who had been languishing, regrouped as the Highwaymen—Willie, Waylon, Cash, and Kristofferson—and took the world by storm. By decade's end everyone was talking about "the Class of '89," the year when Garth Brooks, Clint Black, Travis Tritt, and Alan Jackson made big moves.

I loved and respected all these artists. I learned from them all. When I entered the recording scene in the 1990s, the focus was on Hat Acts. Garth was the best example. He did wear a hat, but he also had a great voice and blended country with rock. Shania Twain also had mammoth success by crossing over from country to pop.

When I came around, my aim was simple: sing great songs, with conviction. I wanted to sing songs that reflected who I was, or at least who I pretended to be. As a man, I obviously contained a million contradictions. But as an artist, I was singularly focused. I'm a proud singer, no matter how messed-up my personal life. If Sony wanted to position me as a full-throated country singer whose songs would also appeal to a pop market, fine; the bigger the market the better.

I'm not proud to say that during this period I recorded my first song—in fact, my entire album—while high as a kite. In all those recording sessions, no one seemed to notice my scabbed nose. I had become a functioning meth head. And, weirdly, I was functioning damn well—at least when it came to singing.

The song Sony/Epic Nashville had chosen, "What Mattered Most," was composed by Gary Burr and Vince Melamed. It was tailor-made for my voice. The story is about a man who, having ignored the emotional needs of his woman, loses her. His inattention to "what mattered most" dooms the relationship. What mattered most was connecting to her heart. What prevented that connection was self-centeredness. Ego blocked empathy. The singer of the song is a lonely, defeated man. Ironically, the lyrics said, "I paid no attention to what mattered most." What mattered most to my own well-being was telling the truth about who I was—and I wasn't about to do that.

The video, shot in Galveston, Texas, has me walking on a deserted beach and gazing at the ocean, driving through the city, wandering through a vacant home, drinking beer in a bar, and all the while catching ghostly glimpses of the woman—a video babe—who has left me.

"What Mattered Most" is the cry of a shattered man. That was a part I could play. Because even though I appeared calm on the outside, my insides were riddled with uncertainty. The song said that I had done something wrong, and I had. I was still doing something wrong. But it was something the world couldn't know about. The world could hear the hurt in my voice, but the source of the hurt remained hidden.

Country music, like so much American music, is based on lamentations. Love found and love lost. Heartache. "What Mattered Most" is powerful country blues, sung by a man who reaches deep into his soul to express excruciating regret.

I felt every word I sang. Fans felt them too. And before the fans, the people at Sony saw it as gold. They were so confident that, in the biggest first-week shipment in the history of Sony/Epic Nashville, they sent two hundred thousand copies of the single to retailers. All two hundred thousand were gone in a flash. "What Mattered Most" rocketed to number one.

I was stunned. I was thrilled. I felt like a fake, but I was determined to do whatever the publicists wanted me to do. Grant interviews. Spread the word. Sell the song. Employ my sparkling personality to win over the world.

Ty at the sold-out showcase performance at Billy Bob's Texas in Fort Worth, Texas, to promote the release of his first album, *What Mattered Most*, to country radio.

The album, also called *What Mattered Most*, kept selling like hotcakes. The second single, "I Want My Goodbye Back," was also a major hit.

The trajectory was straight up. My touring schedule was extensive. Great—because I loved singing to my fans. But not great—because I inevitably got motion sickness on the bus. My loving crew had me stretch out on the back seat and put a wet towel on my forehead, hoping I'd feel better. I never did adjust to the twists and turns of the road.

Nonetheless, I was on a roll and loving it. The adulation made me high. After all those years trying to make it, playing small clubs and cruise ships, I had finally broken through. It was all real, and in my giddiest moments I believed it would keep getting better.

I was managing my life just fine, thank you very much. I had no problem hiding my addiction to porn. No one knew about it, especially not the Cowboy. No one had ever seen the mammoth stash of VHS tapes I'd hidden in a locked closet in Renee's garage. When I was on tour and everyone was off the bus, I would lock the door and hide out there for hours on end, watching porn until my eyeballs bled. If the Cowboy wasn't home, I watched in our den. I had a bunch of secret places where I'd binge. My rationalization was that the only man I was actually touching was me. What was the harm? I never considered the fact that porn was rewiring my brain. Sexually supercharged to start with, I was the last person who needed to get even more sexed-up. I didn't consider the fact that my drive to add fuel to that fire might be part of a larger issue. I told myself there was no harm in what I kept to myself, in the shadows.

CHAPTER 15

CAUGHT

FOR ALL THE thrill of my success, I often feared that I'd be caught in my lies: My marriage to Renee would be seen as a ruse. My relationship with the Cowboy would be exposed. Having reached the top, I'd be brought down by forces outside my control.

That turned out to be true and untrue, all at the same time.

Dallas. Wednesday morning. June 14, 1995. In a secret locale away from the Cowboy. I had been up for two days, indulging in an especially frantic binge of crystal meth and porn. Push in a VHS tape. Take a quick look. "Hey, buddy, I've tricked with you before." Eject the tape. Push in another. Take a hit of meth. Masturbate. Repeat the process until my mind was filled with nothing but graphic sexual images.

And why was I doing this at the very moment that my life was going so well? Shouldn't I have been trying to stay clear for the road ahead? What was I doing? I was doing what all addicts do: creating an alternate reality in which all that matters is the next hit.

Complicating matters more, demands for in-person appearances were pouring in. That very night I was due to play the Texas Police

Association's Centennial Conference in Fort Worth. That meant practically every sheriff in the state would be in the audience. The law was on my side. On the surface, smooth sailing. Below the surface, mayhem. Only someone fully out of control would visit Miss G before a big show. But why not? I loved Miss G. Miss G loved me. A visit to Miss G was always a good thing. My mind was made up.

I put on a tank top, gym shorts, and sneakers before jumping into my pickup to go see my favorite dealer. Miss G always had a quick hit handy. Because Miss G cut my meth with vitamins C and E, I was under the illusion that the stuff was good for my singing voice, when in fact all it did was make my nose drip. Snort a line with Miss G, grab the baggie of dope, and drive over to the dry cleaners to drop off my clothes.

A little while later, I realized I had inadvertently slipped my baggie of dope in among the clothes I gave to the cleaners. When I ran back over to ask if they had seen a baggie of "vitamins," they said no.

Was this a sign from God telling me to slow down? Telling me to forget the drugs?

Yes.

Did I heed the sign?

No.

So, I hurried over to the ATM to pull out enough cash for another buy, then went back over to Miss G's.

"Boy," she said, "you are a mess. You sure you want more?"

"I'll be on the road for six weeks," I said. "I need a good supply."

"All right, baby. I'll take care of you."

Miss G fixed up another batch, cutting the meth with vitamin C. I snorted up a line. I got a jolt. It *was* good stuff. This time I would be more careful. I took a tiny amount and put it in a large Il Bisonte wallet crafted in fine Florentine leather, a gift from Donna Scott. I slipped the wallet into the glove compartment of my truck before driving home to see the Cowboy. The Cowboy was always cool. He was tolerant of those times when I'd disappear without warning. Our house was a place where, after losing my dope at the dry cleaners, I thought I could put the panic away.

"I know you have a gig tonight," said the Cowboy. "So maybe this would be a good time to relax."

I considered the invitation for a few seconds. The Cowboy was right. If I were a normal man, I'd listen to reason. If we were a normal couple, the Cowboy, proud that I was touring behind my first hit album, would come to the show. If we were a normal couple, he would also accompany me on the band bus for the midnight ride back to Nashville, where tomorrow night a thousand guests—including my entire family—would be assembled to celebrate my number one record. But there was nothing normal about our arrangement.

"I need to run out to the venue for an early sound check," I said. "I'll call you after the show, before I leave for Nashville."

The Cowboy just nodded as I jumped into my truck and headed on over to Fort Worth, some thirty miles west of Dallas. I made good time, but as soon as I got off Interstate 30, the truck was sputtering. Thankfully, there was a gas station nearby. I took that as a good sign. It wasn't. It was the worst sign imaginable. That's because, after pulling into the station and filling up, I noticed that I was across the street from a park notorious for gay cruising. I made a split-second decision to check it out. That decision led to my life going up in flames.

I drove into the park and, despite the shiver of nerves I felt pass over my bones, removed my tank top. I took a hit of meth. I walked past the bushes and benches to a secluded glade surrounded by trees. My heart beat wildly when a tall man approached me. The dance was on. The man was movie-star handsome. He looked to be in his early forties. His trousers and T-shirt were skintight. He had thick thighs and bulging biceps. He smiled. He winked. And then he gave the telltale sign: He grabbed his crotch. All systems go. We approached each other slowly. I was aroused and exposed myself. I thought he would do the same, but instead, like a well-rehearsed actor, he said, "This ain't your day, cowboy," before snapping a pair of handcuffs on my wrists.

I thought two things at the same time: *This is going to be kinky* and *Oh shit, he's a cop.* I was praying for the former. I'd had no experience with undercover law enforcement and couldn't imagine that any cop would ensnare me like this. But that's exactly what was happening. My heart sank. I knew that those few seconds would change my life forever.

Dear God in heaven, erase this moment. Please make it not happen. Please stop this. Make this man go away.

I started appealing to the man, pleading with him in a panic. "You don't have do this. You can let it go. I'm an artist. I'm not gay. My wife is pregnant."

"I suppose if I let you go," he said, "you'll give me your autograph and a free record?"

So, he knew who I was. I hoped against hope that would help.

I said, "I can give you free records of every artist on Sony. Free tickets to every concert for life."

He laughed in my face.

I kept pleading with him. "We didn't do anything. Can't we just forget this whole thing?"

His answer was to shove me into the back seat of his unmarked car, a rusty, beat-up Impala with oversized tires. The inside smelled like puke. I couldn't stop shaking. He didn't tell me his name, and I didn't ask. As we drove off, he did say that he was an officer of the law. He stopped his car at my pickup. How did he know where I'd parked? No time to ask him. He rifled through my truck, throwing my shit all over the ground. He returned to his car holding a bunch of my stuff. I didn't see exactly what. I was too frozen with fear to remember that I'd left that Il Bisonte wallet stuffed with dope in the glove compartment.

As we drove off, I kept pleading. "I just had a number one record. My first. This is gonna ruin me. All I did was show you my dick. Is that worth destroying my life? Take me to my tour bus. My guys will tell you that I have a big gig tonight for the police association. Those are your people. Tomorrow I'm flying to Nashville because they're throwing a party to celebrate my number one record. Please, you're making something out of nothing. And that something is gonna kill my career. Have a heart. I'm begging you."

Begging didn't work. Nothing did. He stayed silent. We drove around for what felt like hours. My brain was on fire. At one point I was convinced he wasn't an undercover cop but a homophobic murderer. Where was he taking me? And why wouldn't he answer me? And how could I have been so reckless? Getting high. Going cruising. Getting caught.

The scenario was so horrible that all I could do was return to denial. This wasn't happening. Soon I'd wake up in bed next to the Cowboy and laugh at this stupid dream. But there I was, in the back of that rundown Chevy, driving up that street, driving down this street, driving onto the highway, off the highway, driving through

Arlington, heading toward Dallas, turning west and heading back toward Fort Worth.

At long last I persuaded him to take me to my tour bus and the semi that had arrived from Nashville and parked in downtown Fort Worth near the venue for the police association ball. He'd see that I was telling the truth about that night's gig and that I was the headliner. I was hoping that my status with the sheriffs would put me in his good graces and get me out of this jam.

My tour bus and semi were exactly where I said they'd be. He parked alongside them. There were a ton of cops. My musicians surrounded the Impala and gazed inside. I looked like death warmed over. No shirt, gym shorts, my hands bleeding from the handcuffs. At this point I was seven hours late and the opening act was already onstage. No one had heard from me. Guests were streaming into the venue.

I saw my drummer, David Pinkston, and my first cousin/roadie David Todd. Mike Rogers, the southwest manager for Epic Records, was also standing there.

"What happened?" Mike asked the cop.

No one was allowed to talk to me or even come near the car. I couldn't answer for myself. Couldn't even roll down the window, because I was handcuffed. I felt like a complete and utter fool, helpless and unable to do a damn thing but sit there and suffer the consequences I'd brought upon myself.

A few officers walked over, asking the cop what was going on. I could just make out the conversation.

"What do you have him for?" asked one of the officers.

"Indecent exposure."

The officers paused before reacting. They went back and forth with the undercover cop. I felt competitive vibes between the sheriffs and the cop. No one seemed to like this cop.

"Well," said the older sheriff, "we'll book him on a minor charge and have him out in an hour so he can do our show."

Thank God! I breathed a huge sigh of relief. But as I sighed, I saw a smirk on the cop's face as he reached into the back seat to take off my handcuffs and hand me a shirt. As he drove off, for the first time I saw it there, sitting on his dashboard: my Il Bisonte wallet. Oh, God! Minutes later we arrived at a police station. The sheriffs had gotten there first. What followed was a series of slow-motion moments: I'm helped out of the back seat. I'm led into the station. I can hardly keep my eyes open as someone takes my mug shot. The officers are all being friendly until a female officer holds up my Il Bisonte and starts screaming, "It's now a felony! Put those fuckin' handcuffs back on him!" Then everything becomes a blur as another female officer picks

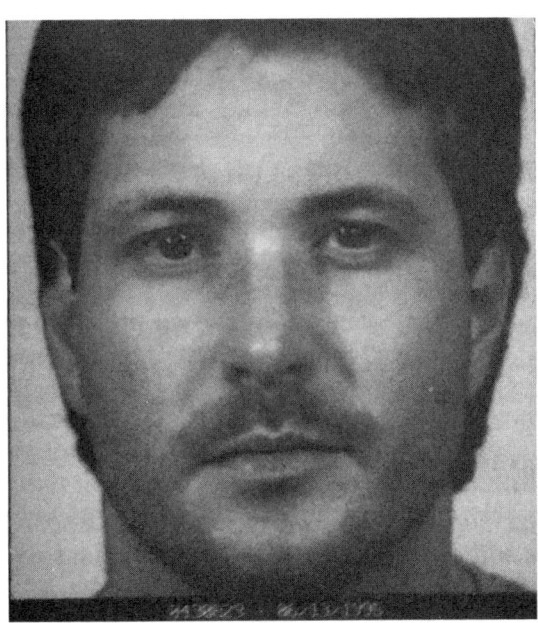

Mug shot, June 13, 1995, Fort Worth Police Department.

up the phone to call a news station about Ty Herndon being arrested, and I'm thrown into a cell alone, with the officers suddenly turning nasty. I'm sitting on a wooden bench, my head in my hands, weeping uncontrollably, until I fall on the floor and curl up in the fetal position. Then I hear a guard speaking to me from the other side of the small slit in the door.

"If you wouldn't mind, Mr. Herndon, my wife would love to have your autograph."

And with that, he slips me my CD—*What Mattered Most*—and a sharpie.

I find the wherewithal to write an inscription, thank the guard, and hand him back the CD.

"Can I bring you a blanket?" he asks.

"That would be great."

The small act of kindness raises my spirit, but not for long.

Fear had me up all night. I didn't know that my good friend Robert Gallagher had come to my aid. Robert managed Billy Bob's Texas, a huge honky-tonk in Fort Worth where I had often performed. He was also promoting the sheriffs' show that night. Robert got me a lawyer and posted bail while Mike Rogers called his bosses back in Nashville to tell them what was going on.

Later, Mike told me that the cop changed his story three different times. In one version, I exposed myself in my truck. In the second, he found me naked while seated on a log. In the third, I coaxed him into following me into the woods. Mike felt certain that the cop was not on the up-and-up.

My management rented a private jet to fly me back to Nashville. By then, the story was everywhere, but it kept spinning in different directions: One version said that a female cop had caught me urinating and, rather than stop, I had blatantly exposed myself to her. The story that stuck said I'd been caught masturbating with another man in public. But the story that saved me from prison was the one registered by law enforcement, which called it a narcotics arrest. That story saved my career, because Sony could say I had a drug problem—a far more acceptable story than one hinting at homosexuality—and I would voluntarily go into rehab.

The morning after my arrest, the news, both accurate and inaccurate, was everywhere. My Alabama family, who had to come to Nashville to attend my number one party, was staying at a downtown hotel. They were called to the lobby and told that the party was canceled due to my arrest. The cause of the arrest wasn't made clear.

Grandma Myrtle stepped forward in her black high heels and said, "It doesn't matter. We're still going to celebrate him. We're going to pray for him. We're going to let him know that his family stands with him. We're going to lunch and will hold our heads high."

The great matriarch led the pack who would not leave Nashville until I was able to show up in person and assure them that I was okay.

I was anything but okay. On the plane from Dallas to Nashville, I was drained. I felt dead. When I landed in Music City, I was able to shower, shave, and change into fresh clothes. If I wanted to salvage my career, though, I was told to report to the Sony offices and apologize. Because the airwaves were so filled with rumors, the execs needed to hear the truth from me, and immediately.

At that point I had been without drugs for seventy-two hours, but I managed to show up. My blue suit was neatly pressed, my white shirt without a stain. I was presentable. After all, I was a performer. My golly-gee nice-guy persona was intact. I was humble and contrite. I said what needed to be said. The sex thing was never mentioned.

Plainly and clearly, in short order, I admitted to being a drug addict who needed help. I committed to going to rehab and to remain there for as long as was required.

When I was through speaking, there was dead silence. I had no idea what the reaction would be. After several nervous seconds, promo team member Paige Connor, whose fiery red hair was the key to her invincible character, ran over and embraced me. We both broke down in tears.

"We're with you, Ty," she said.

Echoing Paige, everyone chimed in.

"We love you, Ty!"

"We're behind you!"

"We're promoting the hell outta your record no matter what!"

What a blessing! This was the day I saw the true heart of Nashville. This incredible team took on a challenge few thought could be met. After my arrest, the industry wrote off *What Mattered Most*. The second single, "I Want My Goodbye Back"—man, the irony of that title!—had been on its way from number five to number one when it tanked. In fact, *What Mattered Most*, programmed to have five number one singles, was written off as a miserable failure.

Yet, miraculously, Epic Nashville saved the day. After the album fell off the top 200 chart, the promo team met one-on-one with dozens of deejays. My label promoters, like the magnificent Mike Rogers, Mark Westcott, and Jack Lameier, argued on my behalf vehemently. "This kid has waited years for this break . . . he deserves it . . . he earned this record . . . he was just in the wrong place at the wrong time . . . besides, he's not gay . . . he's married . . . like half the world, he's just got a drug problem that he's now taking care of. . . ."

Beyond that, they fought the false and nasty rumors being spread by competitor labels: that I had a history of prior arrests; that I'd been found guilty of sexual assault; that weapons were involved. The full force of country music culture's homophobia was aimed directly at me. And yet, because of the promo team's herculean effort, "I Want My Goodbye Back" was resuscitated and climbed back to number five. The album was still alive, and the promotional campaign to save it became a legendary story in the annals of country music.

A label exec summarized their spin: "Ty is getting sober, and all is right with the world."

Nothing would be right—I thought to myself—if my secret stash of gay porn was discovered. Still in a state of trauma/paranoia, I imagined an assortment of scenarios that would prove to the world that I was, in fact, a queer in hiding. So, with my heart beating fast, I called Mom. I told her about the stash. Her reaction didn't surprise me. Mom did what she always does. She protected me. To get rid of my collection, she enlisted the help of Saint Wesley Meyers. It took several trips to the dumpster in their rented U-Haul. Neither Mom nor Wes could believe how much I'd hidden away. When they said, "Mission accomplished," I let out a deep sigh. I was so grateful. Now I could go off to rehab with one fewer worry. Everyone was supportive, especially the Cowboy.

The night I left, I spoke to John Blaylock and Carl Peoples, dear friends from my Opryland days. They had moved to Los Angeles where they were enjoying success, John writing music, Carl producing television.

"Baby," said Carl, "phones are ringing for you all over the country. Positive energy is coming your way. Sony sees you as the next Garth Brooks. So of course they're going to do everything in their power to protect their investment. But, Ty, you have to protect your sanity. You have to take this rehab seriously."

CHAPTER 16

INSTANT REHABILITATION

THE MORNING I arrived at the rehab facility, there was a press conference at the front gate. Now I see that as a horrendous idea. At such a moment, who is capable of speaking coherently? Back then, though, I just went along and did what I was told. Anything to save face. Anything to save my career. I faced a gaggle of reporters and cameras. I spoke briefly. I thanked the promo team and Sony. I apologized to my wife, my mother, and God. Questions were asked, but I can't remember my answers. I was ushered inside.

I did get sober. I met with two counselors every day. Each session was two hours. There were no group meetings. There was no twelve-step work, no connection of recovery to spirituality. I did speak honestly in therapy. I admitted to being gay.

One of my counselors dressed like a cowboy and knew my music. When I told him how I'd been hiding in the shadows of show business, he listened for a long while before he spoke. "It'll be ten years before anyone even begins to forget what happened to you. If you come out, that will only add to the drama. You say you want a superstar career. Well, if you present yourself to the world as a homosexual, that will never happen. Ever. Best you can hope for is a medium career. Very medium."

That got me very upset. Why was a counselor talking that way? Why was he expressing such hopelessness in a setting that was supposed to help me heal?

"I just want you to be realistic," he continued. "You've got a choice. Tell the world you're gay and think about another career, or return to the charade."

I returned to the charade.

The psychotherapy offered in this facility was not profound. There were the inevitable discussions about my upbringing. I never heard the word "trauma." I acknowledged my addiction to meth, but no one suggested that the pornography was also an addiction. No one made the connection that living a double life might be the cause of my need to self-medicate. No one helped me process my rape. Of course, that's because I never talked about it.

During family week, Mom came along with the Cowboy, Renee, Lizard, and Wes Meyers. After my arrest, Wes had been the first friend to call me.

"I feel guilty," he said.

"About what?" I asked.

"I know about those parks. I should have told you to stay out of them."

"I knew too," I said, "but the self-sabotage is on me. Not on you."

"It could have been any of us, Tyrone."

It always helped hearing Wes's voice. I was touched by his willingness to participate in the family group discussion.

The shrink in charge began by talking about my mom and dad. I had told him about my father's alcoholism. As soon as he started questioning Mom, she shut him down. Miss Peggy was there to support me, not to talk about herself or any problems she might have had with her husband.

And so it went. The session was fraught with tension. The shrink didn't really understand my romantic relationship with the Cowboy or my platonic relationship with Wes. Or my marriage to Renee. We just skirted around all the real issues. It was exhausting.

When it was over, the Cowboy, who rarely cursed, told Mom, "I need a goddamn drink." I could only imagine how tough it was for my partner to go through this ordeal. To see him in such pain broke my heart.

Family week was over. The days dragged on. Always the extrovert, I made fast friends with a fascinating cast of characters. My first pal was a woman with an eating disorder. I'll call her Lady 1. Morbid obesity hadn't killed her humor. She was a scream. One day we were sitting by the pool when a new patient arrived, a tall, big-busted blonde stuffed into a Gucci jumpsuit with the double-G logo plastered all over her derriere. I was fascinated by her Cindy Crawford hair and high-heel stiletto slippers.

"I must welcome her," I told Lady 1.

"Why? She's another one of those Beverly Hills bitches who chops up coke while telling her French cook how to season the pot roast."

Ignoring Lady 1, I introduced myself to the new patient, whom I'll call Lady 2, and asked whether I could help her carry her three-piece matching Louis Vuitton luggage.

"Back off, pretty boy," she said, thinking I was making a move. "I'm a fuckin' lesbian."

"Well, I'm a fuckin' fag."

Lady 2 burst out laughing. Lady 1 did the same. From that moment on, we became a trio and spent every evening together laughing and carrying on. Both of these ladies had lived big lives with big problems and were handling them with big humor. Their over-the-top attitudes probably helped me as much as the therapists did. We also bonded with a famous rock star who, to be fair, must also remain anonymous. Though he had a certain charisma and could be fun, he was cynical as hell. When I told him I'd been hooked on crystal meth, he said, "Dude, forget sobriety. That's one drug you'll never get past." Well, that was one thing I didn't want to hear, but I was in no position to argue.

Hints of my life outside rehab kept getting through. For example, when the ladies and I were in line for breakfast one morning, my current single, "I Want My Goodbye Back," was blaring from the loudspeakers. I had to tell my friends it was me, and of course we reveled in the irony of the lyrics, which talked about how a lack of self-control had me on a roll. I also heard the song as a sign that I needed to get back to work. Rather than say goodbye to the Nashville music scene, I needed to say hello.

Both ladies were in disbelief when I showed them the newest issue of *People* magazine. There I was, on the cover with my wife, Renee! The ladies took turns reading it out loud. The piece, cooked up by the Sony/Epic PR team, was all about the remarkable results of my recovery, even though my recovery was still in progress. I was described as an exemplary husband. My comeback from recent misfortune was all but guaranteed. Ty Herndon was as good as new.

Ty Herndon left rehab sober, yet still as confused and lost as ever. It all happened way too quickly. It was like drinking instant coffee. Instant rehab didn't feel like the real thing, but the speedy process allowed me to run back to work and bury my head in the sand. Music would make everything all right. I didn't take the time to truly reflect on why I was doing what I was doing.

* * *

Three days after leaving rehab, I had a sold-out show in Santa Fe, New Mexico, where I walked out to a five-minute ovation. My whole family was there. I couldn't hold back the tears. I told myself that things were better than ever. My voice was strong. On stage, I was in command. Singing "What Mattered Most," I felt that music mattered most. As long as the audience loved me, I could keep going.

My third single, "Heart Half Empty," cowritten by Gary Burr and the mighty Desmond Child, was climbing the charts. A duet with my labelmate Stephanie Bentley, the song laments a lost love.

On my court date for my drug case, the judge invited me into his chambers and asked me to sign a CD for his wife. He then levied one year of probation, a reasonable fine, and a demand that I return to Fort Worth every month to pee in a cup. Given that I'd been caught red-handed, this was a best-case scenario.

Meanwhile, the Epic Nashville PR staff worked overtime, because even if I felt great on stage, the community wasn't fully back on board. There were more puff pieces about the happy Ty-Renee marriage. Though my debut album had yielded three hit singles, my booking agents struggled to get me big venues, so my wagon was hitched to big-name artists for whom I could open. When the arrest happened, I had been slated to tour first with Garth Brooks and then with John Michael Montgomery, but all that went away. We needed a plan B.

Back out on the road, I faced major challenges. The underlying homophobia was unrelenting. A number of country music deejays bought into the story that I had been caught masturbating in that Fort Worth park. They had a field day with "choking the chicken" jokes—Southern slang for masturbating. I tried to laugh it off, but after the hundredth variation of the same stupid joke, I got fed up. I called my buddy Donna Scott to vent.

"I want to kill those assholes," I said.

"Well, you can't do that, Ty. But when you can't beat 'em, just join 'em."

I took Miss Donna's advice and sent taxidermied chickens to five of the biggest culprits with a note that said, "Choke this chicken. Love, Ty."

That's how the chicken-choking joking finally petered out. (Pun intended.)

The scandal sheets at the grocery store checkout counters were more tenacious. One headline said that I was trans; another called me a "country star in ruin."

The only comfort came from my pal Joe Diffie, who said, "Hell, Ty, you should rejoice. Everyone knows that you ain't made it till the *National Enquirer* puts your pretty face on the cover." I tried to cling to the old adage that there was no such thing as bad publicity, but it was tough.

Throughout this whole sordid affair, if there was a measure of revenge to be extracted, leave it to Mom to find the sweetest. Miss Peggy is fierce. Convinced that the undercover cop who busted me hadn't played by the rules, Mom hired a private investigator to check him out. The result was a report containing enough incriminating evidence to get the cop fired. When the cop learned that Mom was responsible for his undoing, he showed up at her door with a gun.

"This double-barreled shotgun is going through this door a lot quicker than your pistol," she said.

The cop turned tail, never to be heard from again.

Life went on. I kept gigging. The crowds were enthusiastic. The venues were growing. The Cowboy and I were cool. My pretend life had me believing that superstardom was at hand.

Then, reality.

CHAPTER 17

"DEATH, BE NOT PROUD"

THE NEWS CAME in a phone call. Renee was seated next to me. Wes Meyers was calling from Fort Worth. He said it so quickly that I wanted to believe I'd misheard him.

"I have pancreatic cancer."

When Renee saw that I couldn't even speak, she reached for the phone. Wes told her exactly what he had told me.

My friend's demise was frighteningly fast.

Wes and I had known each other since we were teenagers, two gay boys looking to make it in the Opryland musical culture, a culture vehemently intolerant of who we were. We suffered in our secrecy, but we also laughed like crazy. We loved singing. We loved entertaining. We comforted and protected each other.

Wes had always been healthy and strong. He had enjoyed a happy domestic life with his partner, Tim, in Fort Worth. He had supported me in every way possible. He supported my wife. Now it was our turn to support him.

It was alarming. He lost his hair. He lost his muscularity. He went from 180 to 80 pounds in the blink of an eye. He soon appeared skeletal. At one point he was unable to eat or even to swallow.

"We both believe in a God of miracles," I told him.

"This time, Tyrone, there'll be no miracles." He could barely whisper—a voice that once could project to the very last row of the biggest concert hall in Opryland.

"*You* are a miracle," I assured him. "You're a miracle of love."

He broke down crying.

"Cowboys don't cry," I said with a forced smile.

He offered me a forced smile of his own and said, "Stop that shit."

During one of our last visits, he was in bed. He asked me to lie next to him. I gently put my arm around him. His frame was frail. His cheeks—and mine—were wet with tears. His breath was labored. Neither of us knew what to say. I could feel his desperation. He didn't want to die. It was far too soon. I kissed his forehead. I kept telling him how much I loved him. How much he was loved.

I had to leave for a gig. That was a Tuesday. On Saturday Renee called. Renee, who had become a loving and devoted caregiver alongside his own family, was with him when he took his last breath.

The aftermath was rough. The Mormon church, having learned of his lifestyle, refused to bury him in the holy vestments he had earned after completing two missionary trips. Wes's mother bravely protested. Fortunately, she prevailed. He was garbed in sacred gowns. Above his grave a gas flame burns eternally. His light cannot be extinguished.

After Wes's transition, a friend read me a poem that had been written by John Donne nearly four hundred years ago:

Death, be not proud, though some have called thee
Mighty and dreadful, for thou art not so;

For those whom thou think'st thou dost overthrow
Die not, poor Death, nor yet canst thou kill me.

As a child, I was taught that love defeats death. I was taught that life does not end in the tomb. Jesus dies to give us eternal life. These were ideas I clung to with all my heart. My mother, who had great love for Wes, understood the depths of my grief and stood with me. So did Renee.

Yet my spirit turned dark. My depression was profound. This was my first friend to die. I'd like to think that shame hadn't surrounded his passing, and yet I knew that, for all our progressive thinking, shame had assaulted us both. We joked about being straight-acting butch cowboys. We tried laughing away the stigma attached to our queerness. But because our queerness had always lurked in the shadows, shame was a constant companion for both of us.

I don't know whether it was shame or fear that, for years after Wes's death, helped me curb my drug use. I stayed faithful to the Cowboy. Despite what looked like an uptick in my career, it was tough to be happy.

CHAPTER 18

LIVING IN A MOMENT

THAT'S THE NAME of my second album for Epic Nashville. It dropped in 1996. It's also the name of the first single from that album, which became my second number one hit. The label was adamant about keeping my career alive. They financed a highly romantic video shoot in the San Antonio train station featuring me and, as my love interest, the blindingly beautiful Donna Scott, who would star in a number of my videos.

When the song went to number one, I finally had the lavish party that had originally been planned for "What Mattered Most." It was a huge affair.

Even though I wasn't allowed to pick any of the songs for *Living in a Moment*, I was grateful that the record execs wanted new music out as soon as possible. The idea was to remind the public that my claim to fame was my voice, not my arrest. I was living in a moment when I still believed that my arrest would just be forgotten. I wasn't so lucky. The nasty jokes never stopped. On a regular basis, some gossip columnist or deejay would remind readers of my murky past or my rumored sexuality with some snarky, off-color comment.

At the same time, with an ever-growing inventory of hits under my belt, I could work as much as I wanted.

On one tour, LeAnn Rimes opened for me. Then, when she broke with "Blue," a huge hit, her management respectfully asked to rearrange the billing. I didn't mind at all. I'd known LeAnn since she was a little girl. I loved her and was happy to have her headline. During my set, she'd always come out and sing a duet with me. Given the sudden surge in her career, we were soon playing arenas. And, bless her heart, LeAnn took me along for the ride.

I was hopeful that other headliners—Garth or Alan Jackson or Wynonna or Shania—might invite me to open for them, but none of those superstars made the offer. The stigma surrounding me was still there. Yet I worked my ass off, playing fairs, festivals, and casinos from Oklahoma to Ohio.

Touring is a blessing—I get to sing for the people—but it's also a bitch. Like the previously mentioned motion sickness. Or the time my

Ty and Donna Scott on the set of the "I Have to Surrender" video in 1996.

bus rode off without me. It happened because the driver had failed to see that, at a rest stop, I'd put a sheet of paper on my seat indicating that I'd gone to the restroom. By the time I was finished, I saw the taillights of the bus way off in the distance. It was cold as hell and I was wearing only a T-shirt, sweatpants, and flip-flops. I had no phone or wallet. I ran into the rest stop attendants' office to tell them to call the state troopers. They looked at me like I was a homeless bum and told me to get out. What the hell was I supposed to do?

I walked around looking for someone who'd let me us their flip phone. One trucker slammed his door in my face. Another roared off without bothering to say no. That's when a lady trucker took pity on me. I was hopeful when I saw a tattoo of Wynonna on her forearm. Before I started explaining my dilemma, she stopped me and said, "I know who are, baby. I'll help you any way I can."

Catching up to my bus took some time. All my bandmates were asleep, and my driver had driven for three hours before realizing I wasn't on board. It was hell reaching him—those primitive cell phones kept malfunctioning—but when I did, we picked out an exit 150 miles up the road where my lady trucker/savior was kind enough to drop me off. In the meantime, she'd been chatting on the CB with another trucker.

"Got me some precious cargo," she said. "I got Ty Herndon riding shotgun!"

"Ty Herndon!" shouted the man. "I love that son of a bitch. He can really sing!"

"Well, if you want an autograph, I can arrange it."

"Hell yes, I want his John Hancock."

The happy ending was also a happy beginning. When we met my bus at the designated exit, my second trucker fan was waiting too.

I grabbed merch from my bus and autographed everything I could for both truckers. They were tickled pink. I was tickled pink when the lady trucker got back in touch with me a month later to say that she and the male trucker had hit it off that night—so much so that they got married and drove off into the sunset!

* * *

Big Hopes was both the right and wrong title for my third album, released in 1998. Professionally, it was right. I did harbor big hopes, and for good reason. I kept having hits. Personally, it was wrong, because my hopes for sustaining two of my primary relationships were waning.

"Big Hopes" was also the title track, written by Walt Wilkins, who tapped into my heart and mind with the line "I got a box of hurt and a bag of shame."

I wanted to write the songs for the album, but the label chiefs refused. They just wanted me to sing. At least they let me pick out most of the songs. Well, actually, I've gotta give credit to the remarkable lady who showed me how to pick songs: Mom.

As usual, Epic Nashville had given me a bucket of songs to listen to. I was over at Mom's going through them in my usual speedy fashion, rejecting one after the other.

"Hold up," she said, "you're going too fast, son. What's wrong with that last one?"

She was referring to a song I'd nixed after I listened to the first verse.

"Ty," she continued, "you gotta learn to listen to music as good as when you sing music. Go back and listen to that whole song."

The song was called "A Man Holdin' On (to a Woman Lettin' Go)."

The opening lines describe two young lovers, their bodies afire, set to swim "a river of desire." I wondered if Mom was thinking about her first encounters with Dad. Whether it was personal for Mom or not, her assessment was right. Hearing it in its entirety, I realized I'd been too hasty in chucking it. It was good enough to record. And when I did record it, Mom's instincts were further validated: It went top five, along with another single, "Hands of a Working Man." The third single, "It Must Be Love," went to number one. I was gratified by these hits but convinced that the biggest hit of all would be the title track. The label refused to release it as a single.

"It's a surefire Grammy winner," I told my A&R boss.

"After all the negative publicity you've endured," he replied, "be grateful that we've promoted three songs. Your fan base will never buy into a fourth single."

And of course we'll never know, because, my arguments be damned, a fourth single was never released.

I was quickly losing hope about my domestic situation. I loved the Cowboy. I will always love the Cowboy. He was the first great love of my life. In my conflicted imagination, he and I would be together forever. But just as my career felt like it was moving in the right direction again, his was moving dramatically down.

When he had to sell his aunt's estate and Highland Park home, I bought a new brownstone on Ross Avenue in East Dallas. I hoped the energy of an urban neighborhood would lift the Cowboy's spirit. I was wrong.

I was also wrong that Renee would remain happy in her role as my wife. She didn't. I was largely absent from her life, and though everyone had agreed to the arrangement, things were strained. There was jealousy between Renee and the Cowboy. Renee wanted more of my time and attention. Remember, I loved both of these people. They were two of my closest friends. The fact that we were enmeshed in a conspiracy of deceit made us all crazy.

Though Miss Peggy was far from crazy, she could also be unpredictable when it came to defending her children. She gives "Mama Hen" a new meaning! I took her to a party in Nashville for the Dixie Chicks (now known as The Chicks), friends of mine who had become the hottest country group in the nation. They were celebrating *Wide Open Spaces*, their first number one album. This was five years before they criticized America's invasion of Iraq and were fiercely canceled for doing so. But on this night in the late nineties, I loved welcoming them into the number one club and introducing them to Mom. After they received their platinum record, I was approached by Allen Butler. I introduced him to my mother as the man who first signed me to Sony.

"Allen," I said, "thanks for all the promo help."

"Don't thank me," he said brusquely. "I was in Europe when you were arrested. If I'd been here, I would have kicked your ass off the label."

And with that, he walked away.

Mom was pissed. She went after Butler and cornered him, waving her finger in his face. I never knew what she told him. She did tell me, though, that "if that's how the head of the label talks to you, son, I'm thinking you'll soon be looking for another label."

Mom's timing was off by only a couple of years.

Steam was my fourth and final album for Sony. It should have been called *Steamin' Mad*. The label insisted on a new version of me. Although I was never overweight—I liked looking muscular—they urged me to diet. They hired a stylist who fashioned my hair with blond tips. The label said I needed a makeover.

I knew that I didn't want a makeover. A makeover would bring attention that I didn't need. If I needed a makeover, it must have been because my image was problematic, right? The change would bring scrutiny. Scrutiny could uncover my secrets. Just let me be a country boy who sings country songs. But that country boy still wanted superstar success, and I figured Sony knew better than I did. I went along with the program. The program also meant that, again, I would sing songs written by others, not by me. This time the program also meant that an A&R man and a producer would select those songs, not me.

Steam generated three singles that went top ten. Sales were robust. Since Sony was allowing me to essentially do an album a year, I had hopes that the label might stick with me. When they started calling me "the Ricky Martin of country music," I could hardly object. This was 1999, the year of Ricky's "Livin' la Vida Loca" (cowritten by my friend Desmond Child). He sold millions of records.

At the same time, I felt like a musical robot. Something or someone

Ty and Mama Peggy in front of his tour bus in 1997.

was controlling me. I sure didn't feel in control of myself. Nonstop shows. Making good money. Sending good money to the Cowboy. Sending good money to Renee. Sending good money to Mom, because Mom was my main emotional support. Sending good money to Grandma Myrtle, just because I loved her. Giving good money to practically anyone with a halfway decent hard-luck story.

The money didn't mean anything to me. I hardly kept track of it. I was in a daze. Record. Travel. Perform. Repeat.

My forever friend Carl Peoples was producing the show *DJ Games* for the Game Show Network. The winning contestants got to attend a concert that became part of the broadcast. Carl arranged a segment where the prize was a front-row seat at a Ty Herndon show. That meant great exposure for me, all thanks to Carl's devotion.

"How are you doing, Ty?" Carl asked me while we were prepping the show in Dallas.

"Couldn't be better."

"Don't give me that sunshine shit," Carl retorted. "You don't look like you're in good shape."

"I can fake it."

"That's the problem," said Carl. "You can fake anything. You can fool anyone. You can fool me, and I'm your brother."

Fooling folks was my superpower, but it was getting harder to fool myself about the tension between the Cowboy and Renee. They both called me incessantly. They both sought my attention. A day didn't go by when one didn't bad-mouth the other. The rivalry was red-hot.

To be in the same room with them was torturous. My way of handling it was to stay out on the road. My justification was that I needed to make money. But who was getting more of my money—the Cowboy or Renee? I hardly knew. I didn't keep up with things like that.

I felt trapped in a life of my own making. That's why, when someone came along with an escape route, I was jubilant. For all the turmoil of my life, jubilance remained my default. I'm a naturally happy man who found himself in unhappy circumstances. I believed in my talent. I believed that my career, despite everything, could still take off like a rocket. I was vulnerable to hype.

CHAPTER 19

HOLLYWOOD

AT THE START of the new millennium, I was thirty-eight. Seventeen years had passed since I was assaulted during my stint on *Star Search*. That was enough time to fool me into thinking that the painful episode no longer mattered. Los Angeles seemed safe again, especially since I had so many trusted friends who lived there.

Donna Scott had become an Angeleno. She was happily married to Tony Scott. They had two beautiful homes, one on the beach in Malibu's Colony and another on Tower Drive in Beverly Hills. Donna always welcomed me with open arms.

So did two openly gay men. Tim Aldrete had a management company and Kevin James was an attorney I'd met in Dallas years earlier. Both were highly successful, and both were fans of my music. In their company, I could relax and be myself. Tim and Kevin were refined, intelligent, and in no way toxic. No drugs, no sex binges, no volatility. They were centered and, by treating me with love, made me feel centered in their presence. In the privacy of their lovely homes, I spent dozens of carefree evenings fooling myself that I could also be an openly gay man.

At a dinner party thrown by Kevin at his elegant Laurel Canyon home, I was seated next to Dana Miller, a mogul who had amassed great power in the entertainment world. Kevin introduced him as the owner of Entertainment Radio Networks. He oversaw many syndicated shows. He was what I call LA handsome—well-tanned, in shape, with a ready smile.

"Dana manages Rick Springfield," said Kevin.

"And I also managed Andy Gibb, may he rest in peace," added Dana.

Kevin was about to tell Dana about all my successes when Dana stopped him.

"I know exactly who Ty is," he said. "I know his hit records. But I also know he's a star who deserves to be a much bigger star."

Suddenly Dana Miller was my best friend.

"Dana Miller," Kevin later told me, "is a great salesman."

Well, I was there to be sold. Dana was a fast talker and a shameless name dropper. I didn't mind. He knew everyone who was anyone in the gay community. Later I learned that that was because Dana was chairman of the AIDS Project Los Angeles. Founded in the early eighties, APLA was nationally recognized as a fundraising force that fueled organizations serving those suffering with AIDS. Dana's commitment to the cause was personal. His longtime partner had died of the disease.

None of this came up during our first meeting. That talk was all about Dana's power as a talent manager. His pitch was direct: He had the pull to cross me over from country to pop. He also had the pull to put me in the movies.

"With that great voice of yours, Ty, with your good looks and natural charm," he said, "there's no reason why you shouldn't be the Next Big Thing."

That's what I wanted to hear. Yet I had to wonder whether this was simply idle dinner party talk. Would I ever hear from Dana again?

I would. The very next day, Dana called to invite me to lunch. A week later, I showed up at his home in the Malibu Colony, just down the street from Donna and Tony Scott. We sat on Dana's deck as his cook served us salad and sea bass. The sun was ablaze, the ocean a sheet of glittering glass. Seagulls soared.

Dana spoke about his history. He'd worked with Bob Hope; he managed Corey Hart; he went on and on until the phone interrupted him. It was Olivia Newton-John calling from Australia.

"Anything for you, sweetheart," he said. "Your favor is granted. I'll speak with Spielberg first thing tomorrow."

Dana turned his attention back to me. He explained the reach of his radio programming, which included big-time shows like *Entertainment Tonight*.

"You can keep your current manager," he said. "If you want to continue operating on the margins of show business, retain your team. But as I see it, Ty, your team is weak. You're a major artist with a minor career. How did that happen? Well, we could analyze that for hours, but analysis will get us nowhere. Better to face facts. The fact is that America has yet to fall in love with Ty Herndon. That's only because no one has had the keys to open the right doors for you. I possess those keys. Let me use those keys. Let me open those doors. Let me turn you into the superstar you were meant to me."

Who could resist that kind of talk? Certainly not me. And certainly not at that moment, when during that same conversation Dana had to excuse himself to take another call. It was Elton John. After their long chat, Dana explained that he and Elton were as close as brothers.

"One final question, Ty," said Dana. "Do you have any reservations about making a clean sweep and launching your career anew from LA?"

"My ties to Nashville are deep," I said. "Label, management, publicity. Pulling out of my Nashville commitment won't be easy for me."

"You won't have to do a thing," Dana promised. "I'll fly to Nashville and have you free as a bird within a week. Leave Nashville to me."

Dana read my mind. I didn't have the heart to fire people, but Dana did. Dana was brash. He spoke about the Gay Mafia in Hollywood and the influence they wielded. He dropped names like Sandy Gallin, who'd managed everyone from Cher to Michael Jackson. Among his close associates were David Geffen, who'd gone from agent to label owner to billionaire, and Barry Diller, who'd conquered the world of entertainment and amassed several fortunes.

Dana did more than sell me. He dazzled me. Perhaps I should have seen a red flag when he mentioned that he'd worked closely with Sam Riddle—the same Sam who'd told me to forget being raped. I had no problem ignoring what should have been a warning sign. I should have seen many warning signs during those early years in LA, but my eyes were closed. Dana used my ambition to win me over—a common move for managers like him.

Initially, Dana also got me good press. Some of it was ridiculous, but I wasn't complaining when Renee and I were featured on the TV show *Lifestyles of the Rich and Famous*. We were seen as a happily married couple and owners of a sprawling cattle ranch in Texas, a wild fabrication. It was also Dana who got me on *Donny & Marie* and *Hollywood Squares*.

Dana did far more than impact my professional life. It was at one of his star-studded parties that I met the man who, at the start of the new century, would dominate my personal life. I'll call him Suave. He was six-foot-two and easy on the eyes, with a big chest, a taut waist, dimpled cheeks, and a chiseled chin, straight-acting but openly gay. Exactly my type.

After the party, Dana suggested that he, his husband, Suave, and I drive into Boystown in West Hollywood, the center of LA's gay nightlife. We went to a few clubs where Suave lavished attention on me. I reciprocated. We talked and laughed, and at one point we kissed. For me, kissing is key. I judge all potential relationships by the power of a kiss. I realize there are better criteria, but at that point in my life, a kiss was the single act I trusted most. Well, kissing turned out to be Suave's superpower. As our lips met, I melted. When our tongues touched, I melted even more. My fate was sealed.

And the end of the night we wound up at his place. Two days later, we went on a formal date. In the flush of our first sex, I wondered if this thing was purely physical. It wasn't. Suave had a disposition that I found soothing. I loved how he opened the car door for me. Loved how he took me to an elegantly understated restaurant in the Hollywood Hills. His cologne had notes of night-blooming jasmine. He was scintillating; he was fresh; he was curious about every aspect of my life and career. He was easy to talk to and had a fabulous sense of humor.

I told him about the Cowboy and how our relationship was in ruins. I told him I was fed up with Dallas. I told him I was changing management. He thought Dana Miller was a great idea. A little later, I soon learned that Dana did not think Suave was a great idea. Dana detested Suave. But Dana's disapproval had little to do with Suave's personality.

Suave quickly won me over. Within a month, he uttered the magic words: "I love you, Ty."

"Well, gosh . . . I love you too," I replied.

I immediately flew back to Dallas, where I told the Cowboy I was going to have to sell my brownstone.

"Why?" he asked.

"I've met someone."

Dead silence. He didn't see it coming.

"Where are you going to live?" he asked.

"LA."

That was it. He was wounded, but I was in no state to attend to his wounds. I just wanted out. We never discussed or even attempted to understand the complexities of our relationship. In the beginning, the Cowboy had made me feel safe. He was my security. He left his wife for me. We had lived in a beautiful home in a beautiful neighborhood. But our lives had been shadowed by secrecy. It was never going to be forever.

As he sat on the edge of our bed and pleaded for me to stay, I removed myself emotionally. The scent of a cheap cinnamon-scented candle filled the room. Like our relationship, the candle was about to go out. I couldn't dwell on this ending. If I did, I might get sentimental and balk. I had to get away. I was spent.

"Don't you have anything to say?" he asked.

I shook my head.

Shocked and devastated, the Cowboy said he would never speak to me again. I couldn't blame him. I was callously leaving a man I loved. I was destroying something precious; I was destroying his love for me. I left him with the carnage. Only now, as I write this book, am I finally able to fully grieve the loss of this relationship.

Renee was indifferent to the move. Our lives had been running on different tracks for years.

I was headed to Hollywood.

* * *

Upon my arrival, Suave revealed his true nature. The fact that I had been blind to it speaks to my emotional ignorance. The incident was hardly subtle.

I got back to LA a day earlier than planned. I wanted to surprise Suave. At that point he was living in the Valley, where he shared a house with a female roommate. When I showed up, around 10:00 p.m., she said that Suave had gone out with friends but should be home soon. She assured me that he would be thrilled to see me.

Hours passed. It was 2:00 a.m. when I looked out the window to see him arrive in a taxi with another man. I figured it was just a friend. To surprise Suave, I hid in his bedroom closet. The bigger surprise came when Suave and his friend entered the bedroom and I heard Suave say, "Let's fuck." Peeping through the closet door, I waited till they were naked before emerging.

Suave showed no remorse. He just smiled and said, "Well, Ty, we never did discuss monogamy. So, since you're here, why not join us?"

I flat-out refused. As did Suave's "friend," who quickly dressed and left.

"You ruined what could have been a perfectly good time," was Suave's response.

He wasn't angry, just bemused. He couldn't understand why I hadn't wanted to join in the fun. For a long while, I sat on the bed and said nothing. Seeing Suave naked always excited me, and this time was no different. Putting aside my lust for a minute, I considered what he'd said about monogamy. He was right. We'd never mentioned it.

"I agree that we had no agreement," I told him. "But going forward, I'd be more comfortable with a commitment. No outside lovers. Is that okay with you?"

"Sure thing, Ty."

He wrapped me in his arms, we made love, and that was that. For many months I put the incident out of my mind. That was easy to do. Suave and I were committed to monogamy. Then he suggested that we buy a house together. Hell yes! A new home with a new man meant a new life in this new millennium. Everything about California was new for me, including and especially my new career—which, according to Dana Miller, would soon be realized.

The house was a brand-new three-story modern stucco structure in Whitley Heights, high in the hills above the Hollywood Bowl. It was perfect for parties. The view was spectacular. I'd profited from the sale of my Dallas townhouse and had money for half the down payment. Suave provided the other half. He was so eager for me to move that he paid for the truck to haul all my furniture from Texas. The furniture fit perfectly. It was all picture-perfect. Suddenly I was living the dream: gorgeous boyfriend, gorgeous home, gorgeous gay life.

I can't accurately say how long the gorgeousness lasted. Was it two years? Or three or four? It's all a blur. I ask myself now: Did I feel any remorse about leaving my team in Nashville after they had done so much to save me during my post-arrest period? Or was my strategy of emotional survival based on avoiding all rearview reflection? Was it too painful for me to examine my past? Of course. It was easier to plunge into a future that seemed filled with promise. Indeed, upon my departure from Nashville, a dear friend had said to me, "If anyone deserves a brand-new day, it's you."

Suave and I had fabulous parties. LeAnn Rimes came to dinner. On summer nights, the music from the Bowl wafted onto our patio; I heard the sweetly soulful Bonnie Raitt singing "I Can't Make You Love Me," a song so beautiful I swore I would record it. The second time Bonnie played the Bowl, Suave bought us tickets and got us backstage to meet Ms. Raitt.

Suave could be brazen without losing his suaveness. I adored him. Oh, the dangers of adoring stunningly beautiful men!

One particularly dangerous moment came when Suave invited the Cowboy to Los Angeles without my knowing. It happened when Suave and I were at Tony and Donna Scott's house in Malibu. During lunch, the door opened and in walked the Cowboy. I was floored.

Donna looked at me and mouthed the words "What the fuck!" before going over and hugging the Cowboy, whom she considered an old friend. The Cowboy completely ignored me. It was beyond awkward. Small talk. Lots of painful silence. At one point Suave made a grand gesture by coming over to where I was seated, taking me in his arms, and kissing me full on the mouth. Seeing that, the Cowboy left abruptly. He had been there for less than an hour.

Incensed, I asked Suave to walk with me on the beach. I needed a private talk.

"What the hell was that all about?" I asked.

"Well, you once loved him. I thought you'd want to see him again."

"No, you didn't," I insisted.

"Yes, I did."

"Come clean."

"I wanted to see how handsome he was," said Suave.

"I already told you that. Besides, you've seen pictures."

"I thought it'd be fun to see him in person."

"Fun?" I asked.

"Yes, fun. If he hadn't run off, I was going to invite him to spend the night."

"For a threesome?"

"Ty, you have such a wild imagination," he said.

I changed subjects and never brought it up again. I should have. I should have voiced my doubts about Suave's honesty. But those were doubts I wasn't prepared to entertain. All doubts were suppressed by the power of our lovemaking and the beauty of my new, out life.

As Suave put it, he was interested in having "a devilishly good time."

One of the greatest times involved Mom and Aunt Greta. Suave, who loved international travel, invited them to join us on a trip to Amsterdam. They'd never been to Europe before and had a ball. They saw their first gay bar and danced with beautiful men at the discos. The most stunning moment came while we were walking through the red-light district, where the lady prostitutes wore fetching lingerie and sat in the front windows of their apartments, which were decorated with elaborate curtains, rugs, and furnishings.

"Oh, this will never do," said Aunt Greta as she stopped in front of a window where a woman was seated in a plain chair. Her nightgown was tattered and her surroundings bare. Greta knocked on the window and signaled for the lady to come out.

When my aunt offered her money, the woman thought that she was being hired. "Oh no, honey," said Greta. "I just want you to buy yourself something nice. A pretty robe, a dainty table, and a fancy lamp."

She graciously accepted my aunt's offering.

Before leaving Amsterdam, Greta insisted that we return to visit her friend. When we did, my aunt was pleased to see that the lady of the night had put the money to good use. Her revealing lingerie was new—as was the purple velvet love seat upon which, her long legs crossed, she was now perched.

Seeing Greta, she blew her a kiss. Greta smiled and waved.

"I love this city," said my aunt.

Mom nodded in agreement.

CHAPTER 20

"THE GOOD LIFE"

THAT'S THE NAME of a standard that speaks to my heart, whether it's sung by Tony Bennett or Ray Charles. It's a lament, a reflection on the impossibility of realizing romance. I also hear it as an unanswered prayer. The good life is elusive. It sure has eluded me. I thought I had it. I thought Suave was the Good Life. I thought Dana Miller was the Good Life. California just had to be the Good Life.

How could I have been so wrong? After all, back in Dallas, Renee was still my wife . . . at least for now; I still wanted the world to think that I was straight. I still thought I could live the Good Life even while living two lives at once.

I also wanted to believe that my new relationship with Suave would be forever. It would blossom and grow. During our big parties, if a group of sophisticated gay men were down in our garage doing some lines of meth, I took a snort. Only a tiny amount. A nip here, a nip there . . . I could handle it. Another illusion I needed to believe in.

On the career front, it made no difference when word went out that Sony was dropping me, although I was contractually guaranteed two more albums. It made no difference because Dana Miller had convinced me that I should leave Sony anyway. He promised that he could take me from country stardom to pop stardom, which Sony would never do. And soon Nashville was abuzz with a new lie concocted by Dana: that I had walked out on a coveted record deal with Sony because other labels were hot to sign me. I believed Dana when he said he'd set up meetings with powerful label heads, movers and shakers like Mo Ostin and Jerry Moss. Yet none of those meetings happened. And the one that did happen—with Elton John—was unpleasant to the extreme.

Dana took me to one of Elton's big AIDS dinners. I had high regard for Elton's dedication to the cause. He had been a vocal and effective champion for the gay community for decades. I wanted to tell him that but didn't get a chance. When Dana introduced me, Elton said snidely, "Oh, you're the *cunt*-try singer."

"I don't usually identify myself that way," I replied, "but I am a damn good country artist."

Elton looked the other way, flashed a quick smile, and left to mingle with other guests. I was mortified. Only later did I learn that Elton held great disdain for Dana. Yet in Dana's mind, he and Elton were close buddies. The same delusion carried over to Dana's relationships with those label heads. I don't want to admit how long it took me to realize that Dana didn't have any juice with them. It wasn't just months that I stuck with a manager who wasn't who he pretended to be. It was years. I think back now and feel horrified by my naïveté. Or maybe I just needed to go along because it all fit with the illusion of my fake life. In the beginning, life with Suave was exciting, even idyllic. Yet his attitude—that it was okay to do a smidgen of drugs now and then—convinced me of the same. Mixed in with the occasional drugs were the occasional threesomes, which, it turns out, were high on the list of Suave's sexual preferences. I went along more often than I felt comfortable doing. I really only wanted Suave, but I feared that denying him the pleasure of a threesome might turn him against me—and I couldn't deal with that prospect. Better to close my eyes and participate in sexual scenarios that always left me feeling bad. Increasingly, I numbed myself with drugs. And though I'd like to say it was Suave's fault, it wasn't. I liked dipping and dabbing with mind-altering substances. I alone made the choice to get high. I was still an addict.

* * *

God bless Carl Peoples, who witnessed all this with loving patience. I was gigging in Arizona when he came along to make sure I was okay. I'd tried to hide the fact that I had begun using again, but on this weekend even I couldn't camouflage my high. I was taking hits off all kinds of shit.

Naturally I denied it, and, because Carl aways knew how to handle me, he accepted the denial rather than risk confrontation. He dropped me off at my hotel, where I would bathe and dress for my show.

As soon as I was alone in the room, I broke out the goods and snorted up a mess of crystal meth. To take the edge off, I decided to get into the bath. The idea of soaking my overheated body in an overheated bath was irresistible. I remember how I carefully stepped into the tub—I was aware of the danger of falling—but I ignored another, more perilous danger: falling asleep.

Had it not been for Carl, I would have preceded Whitney Houston in death by drowning in a hotel bathtub. It was only Carl's conscientiousness about checking up on me that saved me. When he opened the bathroom door, my head was underwater. He climbed in, pulled me out, resuscitated me, and managed to get me dressed.

When we arrived at the gig, Carl went to see Dana Miller and said, "I have your artist in my car, but he will not be able to perform. He's out of it. He doesn't know where he is. Thirty minutes ago, he nearly drowned to death."

"Oh, that's nothing," said Dana, according to Carl. "He'll be fine."

Carl was infuriated by Dana's reaction.

"I gave that man hell, but he turned out to be right," Carl later told me. "The minute Dana took you into the wings, your instincts took over. You went out there and killed. The show was phenomenal. You pretended like nothing was wrong. You're the Great Pretender."

At some point, though, I could no longer pretend. That's when I decided that if I was going to be bad, why not take it all the way?

Even an idiot would realize that ingesting a bit of meth now and then would only lead to full-blown abuse. An idiot would also realize that once Suave and I started getting high and introducing third parties into our bedroom, my drug addiction would trigger my sex addiction.

It should have been clear that all these addictions were connected—not only to one another but to my bipolarity as well. How could I not have known that I was saddled with an all-or-nothing personality? Give me all the drugs, all the porn, all the partners. Give me everything. The truth was that when it came to getting high on substances or sex, I couldn't ever get enough. But I was blind to the truth.

When it came to Dana Miller, I'd also been blind. Whatever grand illusions I had about the man came crashing down. I shouldn't have been surprised. Carl Peoples had questioned Dana's competence and character from the get-go, but I'd always defended him. Why? Changing management again would be an ordeal. I didn't want any ordeals. I just wanted my perfect LA life to continue.

The ruination of my relationship with Dana was brought on by him, not me. It happened on a day when he'd invited me to his home in Malibu.

Dana was a prince of Malibu. He had the right house, the right view, the right servants. Lunch was always a production. The imported cheese. The fresh fruit salad. The seared salmon. Three flavors of sorbet. And, of course, rare French wines perfectly paired with each course.

I loved Dana's lifestyle. But at this point his failure to deliver on his promises was something I could no longer ignore. I, who hated confrontation, had to confront him. The damning facts about Dana were so blatant that I could no longer ignore them. After taking my last bite of mango sorbet, I turned to my manager and said, "This was such a lovely lunch."

"And you're such a lovely man."

I love compliments, but in this instance I was determined not to be distracted. "Dana," I said, "you've been saying you would line up meetings for us with label heads."

"And I will. But first let's have a bit more wine."

Dana had already downed half a bottle. His words began to slur as he started talking about securing me a record deal by the end of the month.

"Who's going to sign me?" I asked.

"Everyone's gonna want to sign you, Ty. You know that as well as I do."

"All I know is what I see. And what I see is nothing. No meetings. No progress."

Another sip of wine. He was beyond loose. He was tipsy.

"Patience is required," he said.

"I've been patient for more than a year now. My patience has run out, Dana."

"Find a bit more patience, Ty, because . . . well, I'm telling ya, that big breakthrough is almost here."

"I don't believe it."

"Ya gotta believe. Ya been working, haven't you?"

"Small venues."

"You want big."

"Everyone wants big," I said.

"I've heard you're real big."

And with that, Dana's intentions became clear.

"You're not serious," I said.

"Hell yes, I'm serious."

He then began to tell me how much he'd always wanted me.

"So, this is what this whole thing's been about?" I asked him. "This whole fuckin' thing has been about sex?"

The glint in his eye said yes.

That was it. I was out the door.

Goodbye, Malibu.

Goodbye, career comeback.

As I drove back to LA, the traffic was fierce. I was stuck. Stuck in every conceivable way. After all these years in show business, I was still so naïve. Still a pathetic fool. The traffic on Highway 1 wasn't going anywhere. I wasn't going anywhere.

How much time had I spent deluding myself that Dana held my

key to the kingdom? I didn't want to count. I wanted the traffic to start moving, and I wanted my life to move too. Maybe there had been a wreck. My career was a wreck. I could always work because I could always sing. I needed to go home.

But where was home?

CHAPTER 21

"HELP ME MAKE IT THROUGH THE NIGHT"

THAT HAUNTING SONG was written by Kris Kristofferson and turned into a hit by the great country singer Sammi Smith. In 1972, Sammi gave birth to a son she named Waylon. The son's father was Jody Payne, Willie Nelson's longtime guitarist and a fine artist in his own right. Waylon Payne was named for his godfather, Waylon Jennings. Country royalty, Waylon Payne grew up to become a super-talented singer-songwriter. He was also a beautiful man. For a while, he was my man. And as we came together, we both fell apart.

We met in 2002 when I was forty and Waylon was thirty. We met when I was in bad shape. We fell into an addictive love. We became two souls lost in the dark fog of mind-altering drugs.

When I was with Suave, I was living sober—at least at the beginning. But by the time Waylon came along, I was well into a major relapse. Artistically, we formed a mutual admiration society. Waylon never tired of telling me how much he loved my singing. And when I heard Waylon play his guitar and sing his own songs, I returned the praise. We were literally intoxicated with each other. We were Bonnie and Clyde, enabling each other to take more and more risks.

At a party in the Hollywood Hills, my friend, I'll call him Shotgun, a fine country songwriter, introduced me to Waylon, who was living at Shotgun's house. With his big hair, thin, sexy body, and high energy, Waylon was irresistible. He was excited to meet me. He knew my records. I was excited to meet him and learn about his record deal with Motown. We talked music for a while. We learned that we had both been child preachers. We had everything in common. And, in those first moments, we both knew what we wanted.

Back in his bedroom at Shotgun's house, Waylon and I made love. I was still living with Suave but was now hopelessly obsessed with Waylon. I went to Shotgun's house every afternoon to be with Waylon. Suave found Shotgun's address, and one Saturday morning in the pouring rain started banging on the front door and calling my name. I was in bed with Waylon. Waylon jumped up, got dressed, and went to the front door. I did the same. Suave wouldn't stop banging and screaming, *"Ty! Come home! Come home right now!"*

Waylon opened the door and told Suave to go away. Suave wouldn't budge. Waylon pushed him, and they got into a fight that came to a quick halt when Shotgun, a muscular 250-pounder, came out with his shotgun.

"Son," he told Suave, "get off my property or I'll shoot your nuts off."

Watching Suave turn around and leave broke my heart. Of course I was the one who was breaking his heart, and, feeling both his pain and mine, I nearly shouted out, "I'm coming with you, Suave! I made a mistake! I want you back!" But I stayed silent. I wanted Waylon.

Soon, Waylon and I rented an apartment on the eastern edge of Hollywood. After moving in, we learned that Judy Garland had lived there for a year. Her signature was on the wall in the closet. Naturally that thrilled us. I was also thrilled by the velvet drapes in every room. I love a bit of fancy homemaking.

One day I was looking through those drapes and saw Suave standing by his car in the pouring rain. He was sobbing. It wasn't the first time he had come to the apartment, but it was the last. He caught me looking at him. For a moment, I believe he expected me to ask him in. I didn't. He got into his car and drove off. I knew he had given up. It was done. It broke my heart to break his, but I was just too involved with Waylon to look back. Here again, I was leaving the man I had blown up my life for. I was in the throes of a self destructive pattern I was too sick to see.

I called Miss Peggy to say I was doing fine in LA, but from the tone of my voice she knew that I was far from fine. I never gave her the details of my love life. I didn't have to. She could tell that I was out of control. She wouldn't admonish me about getting my act together. That wasn't her style. But I could tell from the tone of *her* voice that she saw me cruising for a bruising. Her silence spoke volumes. She had no fucks left to give at this point.

Waylon and I held a commitment ceremony at Carl Peoples's house and in an altered state, pledged our love and fidelity. We were so convinced our love would last forever that Waylon tattooed "BTH" (for "Boyd Tyrone Herndon") across his belly and I tattooed "WMP" (for "Waylon Malloy Payne") on my arm. A wiseass friend later remarked that his BTH looked like "BITCH" and my WMP looked like "WIMP." Any way you looked at it, we were bonded and branded and hopelessly entwined.

Amazingly, the drug-fueled life didn't seem to damage the music Waylon and I were making. He began work on a new album, *The Drifter*, that turned out beautifully, especially his version of the Shelby Lynne–Glen Ballard song "Jesus on a Greyhound."

"Just because we get high doesn't mean we can't sing," said Waylon, who, for all our unhinged behavior, reminded me that on our worst day we could write and sing our asses off.

Were it not for Waylon, I probably wouldn't have had the confidence to record a Christmas album for a small label, a suite of traditional carols packaged under the strangely appropriate title *A Not So Silent Night*. Not only did Waylon support this effort but he also sang a gorgeous duet with me. Our take on "O Come, O Come Emmanuel" is hauntingly perfect. Musically, we were a magical fit. Even more remarkably, we made this sacred music while we were stoned to the gills. *A Not So Silent Night*—the title song of which was written by Carl Peoples, John Blaylock, and yours truly—should have been called *A Not So Sober Night*.

Morning, afternoon, and night, Waylon and I got higher and higher—high making love, high writing songs, high doing drugs. Inside the Judy Garland closet, we put together some makeshift recording gear. I'd write melodies, and so would Waylon. Waylon would write lyrics, and so would I. One song was about a fool who is so much in love that he's lost all reason; he sees himself as a worthless loser whose only redemption comes through his lover. That was Waylon talking about Waylon; or me talking about me; or us talking about each other. It didn't matter, and we couldn't tell the difference.

Our loved ones grew alarmed. We each had a group of friends who, watching our behavior, were determined to intervene.

In my case, I still feel indebted to Tim Aldrete, Carl Peoples, Donna Scott, and others who tried bringing me back to sanity. It didn't matter how many long evenings they spent arguing that I needed immediate help. Their arguments went nowhere, because my insanity said to ignore them.

Waylon also had a group of buddies concerned about his welfare. His two besties were singers Deana Carter, who hit it big with "Strawberry Wine," and Tonya Watts, who scored with "Alabama Crimson." These were two intense ladies who loved Waylon and staged an intervention to get him into rehab. He went, but two days later he was back in the apartment with me.

Weeks turned into months, months turned into years, and all the while my mind turned to mush. I could still make my gigs, but barely. Waylon kept writing, singing, and performing. But he too was hanging by a thread.

Amy Winehouse's song was a few years in the future, but the sentiment was something I clung to with absolute determination: I wasn't going to the rehab. And there wasn't anyone in the world who could make me.

Except for one person.

CHAPTER 22

MISS PEGGY AND THE COFFIN

TWO WEEKS BEFORE Mom came to rescue me, Waylon and I wrote a song about our inability to stop what we had started. We called it "One More Night." We needed one more night, one more day. When it came to each other, we couldn't stay away. We tried to leave, but couldn't walk out the door. We had to have more, more, more. Not only had we failed to do what we both knew we had to do—split up—we had stopped trying.

During this, the darkest of my declines, my mother was in touch with my friends. But because I was so adept at fooling them, not everyone saw the truth. I hid behind dozens of masks. But Miss Peggy saw right through me. When we spoke, I did my best to sound coherent, but she knew that I was in mortal danger. Her response was unexpected. She hardly said a word. She understood that words were a waste of time. Instead, she flew to LA and turned up at my door alongside Donna Scott. I would later learn that it was Tim Aldrete, Donna Scott, and Suave who had facilitated the trip.

Mom could have said that I looked like hell. That she was worried for me. That she loved me and wanted me to come home. Miss Peggy wasn't about to waste her breath, however. Instead, she handed me a photograph of a coffin.

"That's yours," she said. "I've bought it. I've also arranged for your funeral. You'll be buried next to your grandpa."

Before I could get out a word, she kissed me, hugged me tightly, and left. That night she was back in Nashville.

Miss Peggy's plan ultimately worked. The picture of my coffin was worth more than a thousand words. The notion that she was planning my funeral shocked me to my core. But the shock didn't immediately get me to rehab. Instead, I left LA and followed my mama back to Nashville. I had enough sense—barely—to know I had to leave the place where Waylon and I had lost control. Yet in spite of the fact that friends like Donna and Tim were saying they'd pay for another trip to treatment, I still wasn't ready.

I moved in with Mom. I believed my mother would protect me. But here's the truth that, even now, I hate to disclose: Even after Mom showed me the photo of the coffin and told me of her plans for my funeral, even after I was able to leave Waylon and come to Nashville, I still had drugs surreptitiously sent to me.

I was living in Mom's basement and arguing that I could withdraw on my own while I was doing everything I could to get my hands on high-powered crystal meth. On the day the package arrived from LA, Mom got the mail before me. She opened it and knew exactly what it was. She emptied the meth onto Grandma Myrtle's cake plate, put a glass cover over it, and placed it on the kitchen table. When she called me upstairs, she and my sister Alicia, pregnant with my nephew Jack, were seated at the table with the cake plate in front of them.

With absolute calm, Mom said, "Your sister and I are going to lunch, and when we get back, this has to be gone."

The fact that she didn't chastise me made it that much worse. And yet . . .

I gathered up the meth and smoked half of it. As it entered my body, I felt sick with shame. I took the rest of the shit and flushed it down the toilet. I fell into bed and stayed there for days, racked with self-disgust and depression.

My depression deepened with the news that my friend John Blaylock had died of a brain aneurysm at age forty-three. John and I had bonded at Opryland. He, Carl, and I were the Three Musketeers. We sang, danced, and laughed together. My romance with John was brief, but his bond with Carl was enduring. Their devotion to each other was a model I could never quite attain. That was another personal failure that made me believe my self-loathing was justified. And though that small voice inside me was barely audible, I could hear it: "Listen to your mother. Do what you need to do."

That meant rehab. But who would pay? I couldn't begin to foot the bill. My generous friends offered, but I felt uneasy with such an overture. I had let them down before. I could refuse my friends but I couldn't refuse MusiCares, a wonderful organization that provides for artists who need help.

MusiCares threw me a lifeline. I grabbed hold of it.

CHAPTER 23

"I AM A FAKE"

I WOKE UP realizing that today was the day. I was nervous but ready. I opened the window and breathed in the cool morning air. I could smell the aroma of the coffee Mom was brewing in the kitchen. I packed my bag, got dressed, said a prayer of gratitude, and went upstairs. Mom, Alicia, and my faithful friend Leigh "Lizard" Brannon were there to greet me. I couldn't eat more than a piece of toast. I sipped a bit of orange juice and downed a cup of coffee. Then it was time to pile into the car and get going. Lizard did the driving. I sat shotgun and turned on the radio. The Kendalls were singing their classic "Heaven's Just a Sin Away." God knows that song spoke to me. We all sang along.

As we got closer, my nervousness grew. My stomach growled. What was I doing? I took a couple of deep breaths, closed my eyes, and said another silent prayer: *Dear God, get me through whatever I need to get through.* The place wasn't far outside Nashville proper, though we might as well have been back in Butler, Alabama. The sprawling countryside was lush. The rehab facility, Cumberland Heights, looked like a horse farm. The 177-acre campus sat on the banks of the Cumberland River. Mighty impressive.

A nurse with big energy greeted us at the door of the main building. Now my stomach was in knots. I said my goodbyes to Mom, Alicia, and Lizard and was escorted to my room. That night I met with my main counselor, Regina Taylor, an unapologetic lesbian and big country music fan who was quick to say, "Don't expect any favors." I liked her from the get-go.

It was Regina who got me through Cumberland. She called me by my real first name—Boyd—and dealt out the kind of tough love she felt I needed. In her group sessions, her first question to me was "Who are you?" "A country singer," I said. "I need to stop you right there," she said. And with that she put me in the hall, where she had me wear an "I Am a Fake" sign around my neck.

Regina's strategy was simple: Break me down. Dissipate my shame by exposing it.

At age forty-two, I was still covered in shame. How could it be otherwise? I was still in a fake marriage. I still presented myself to the world as straight. My musical persona had long been fake: a male country singer who sang love songs to women; a male country singer who, in his public presentation, covered up even the smallest hint of homosexuality.

In Regina's group sessions, I didn't cover up. I came out. I said I was gay. That felt good. It even felt great. But I also did so with the understanding that Cumberland would not reveal any private information discussed in the sessions. The same was true with my closest friends. They weren't about to tell the world I was gay, because they understood I still feared doing so would kill my career.

Regina did something similar to what Mom had done earlier: She laid me on the floor, put a black veil over my body to represent a coffin, and had the group mourn me. I was witnessing my own funeral.

She played Vince Gill singing "When I Call Your Name." I broke down into a million pieces.

"Let Old Boyd die so New Boyd can be born," Regina boomed.

At Cumberland, I began to understand the deeply embedded strain of self-hatred that lived inside me. Internalized homophobia. And though it was cathartic to discuss that truth and not view my sexuality in a negative light, no one at Cumberland diagnosed me as suffering from sex addiction. Not to mention love addiction. Or codependency. Or mental illness. It would take years before I faced any of those glaring comorbidities.

Still, Cumberland was the first place I was exposed to twelve-step recovery plans. Maybe because of my strong belief in Christ and because the founders of this model were believers as well, I took to the steps immediately. It didn't bother me that instead of using the word God or Jesus, the nomenclature was changed to Higher Power. The twelve-step wording was designed to attract as many people as possible.

I loved the simplicity of the first three steps:

I admit that I'm an unmanageable mess.

I believe the Spirit can bring me to sanity.

I'll let the Spirit do just that.

It was also good to take a fearless inventory of my shortcomings. Show remorse. Make amends. Help my brothers. Help my sisters. Reach out to those still suffering. And listen. In those group meetings, I got to talk for ten minutes at most. The other fifty minutes I spent listening. Being a righteous witness. Imbibing the pain of others. Learning that my acting out was not unique. Learning that listening to others takes me out of myself and allows me to see that I'm not the center of the universe. Helps me understand how untreated addiction creates a narcissistic bubble that, without deep reflection, cannot burst. Hearing the stories of others fosters reflection. Creates compassion. Creates a community where my story helps heal you and your story helps heal me.

As before, there was a family day. Mom came, but Miss Peggy was never prepared to analyze anyone's psychology, especially her own. When they started talking about the mother-son relationship or the mother-father relationship, my mother still wasn't having any of it.

"I'm glad my boy is here," she said. "And I do hope you can knock some common sense into that thick head of his and help him."

I stayed for the prescribed thirty-four days.

Did Cumberland do me a world of good?

I'd have to say yes, because twenty years later, I'm still steppin' to a twelve-step beat.

I arrived at Cumberland with zero self-worth and left with enough self-worth to keep me going.

And yet my first big move after Cumberland showed that there was still way more work to do.

I went back to Waylon.

CHAPTER 24

WALK THE LINE

WHEN I LEFT Cumberland, I recorded a song called "Ready to Go." The lyrics expressed my heart:

Let the preachers stroll in
Let my new life begin
Let the past burn itself down
I'm gonna break me some new ground
I'll pretend that I'm brave when I'm scared
When I face the unknown
Turn loose of my heart
I'm ready to go
Don't leave me behind

I did feel ready to face life again. Ever the optimist, I saw it as a new life.

And yet, for all that had gone down between us, why did I still want to be with Waylon? After a month of rehab, you'd think I would know not to return to the most turbulent relationship of my life. You'd think I would listen to friends like Donna Scott.

"You're going where?" she asked when I was out of Cumberland and back to living with Mom in Nashville.

"Memphis."

"And why are you going to Memphis?"

"To see Waylon."

"And what is Waylon doing in Memphis?"

"Playing Jerry Lee Lewis in *Walk the Line*."

"And do you know if Waylon is sober?"

"Have no idea. All I know is that Reese Witherspoon is playing June Carter and Joaquin Phoenix is playing Johnny."

"Weren't you guys absolutely toxic together? Going there doesn't seem like an insane thing to do?"

"I have the tools I need not to get high. I can manage it."

Having said those words, I remembered the first of the famous twelve steps: Admit that your life is unmanageable. When I worked that step, I believed it. I couldn't manage my life. But now, back out in the world, I believed things had changed, and that I could manage an unmanageable relationship. Of course I was fooling myself. Of course I was acting impetuously. Of course I was going against the rehab therapists' advice when they told me not to make any major moves for ninety days.

I wanted to see Waylon. And I lacked the strength to stay away. He hesitantly agreed. Even though I knew it was the wrong move. When I arrived, we hugged, but the hug lacked warmth. He was distant. He introduced me to Joaquin Phoenix as a "friend." "Actually," I said, "I'm his husband." I got the feeling that in talking about his life with his fellow actors, I was a mystery.

I confronted him.

"What's going on?"

"I'm working—that's what's going on."

"I mean what's going on between us?"

"Let's talk after this film wraps. Right now, I gotta be the Killer. I gotta be Jerry Lee Lewis."

"I understand, but I wanted to see you."

"I don't have a lot of time, Ty. They're calling me to set."

I left Memphis feeling like shit.

I sought solace from a new friend, Bonnie Hadden, whom I'd met in Augusta, Georgia. I'd been there for a show and had arrived in bad shape. Due to years of meth addiction, I'd ground my teeth so intensely that a couple of crowns had fallen out. The promoter found me a dentist, and, as it turned out, Bonnie was the dentist's assistant. We became instant buddies.

"You can't be a country star with missing teeth," said Miss Bonnie. "You'll look like you belong on *Hee Haw*."

She invited me and my band over to her folks' house for a big ol' country dinner. Ten years older than me, Bonnie became my big sister. She had the sort of Southern family that brought back the best loving memories of my own family. I needed all the love I could get, because that dental work wound up taking weeks and involved serious pain. Bonnie got me through the ordeal.

With my teeth finally fixed, I was planning my next move. I was ready to leave Augusta. If you can believe it, I'd decided to go see Waylon. Again. After *Walk the Line* had wrapped, he'd returned to LA. Now I felt compelled to go to LA.

Bonnie, who knew my long history with Waylon, advised against it.

"You already know how it's going turn out," she said.

"I feel like he needs me," I said. "His mom's sick, and I want to be there for him."

"But from what you've told me, Ty, this seems like a real bad idea." Of course Bonnie was right, and of course I paid her no mind.

* * *

I had a reason to believe there was hope. The film wrapped, and Waylon called to explain himself. Things would be different for us in California.

I wanted to believe him. So, I bought a cheap plane ticket and flew from Nashville to LA.

He said he would pick me up at the airport, but he was nowhere

Ty and longtime friend Bonnie Hadden in Laughlin, Nevada, in 2025.

in sight when I landed. When I called him, he said, "Go back to Nashville, Ty. I think that's where you need to be."

Why should I be surprised? His team saw me as the ex who was wrecking his life and career.

As I began looking for a return flight, my phone buzzed.

It was Waylon.

"Don't leave," he said. "I'm on my way to get you."

Forty minutes later, we were driving to Palm Springs, where his mom was living. The traffic was heavy and the trip took forever. We hardly spoke. Inside the car, the air was stale. Outside the air was thick with smog. I saw the blood-orange sky turn purple as it melted all over Interstate 10. I felt the heaviness of Waylon's heart. He was worried sick about his mother.

When we arrived at Miss Sammi's place in Palm Springs, she was back in her bedroom. She tried her best to put on a good face, but she couldn't stop coughing. It was emphysema. She looked frail, yet she couldn't have been sweeter. She loved Waylon dearly, and Waylon adored her. As she tried to comfort her son, her voice was weak. In my mind, I remembered the strength of her singing voice, the beauty of her songs, and her ability to touch the hearts of millions.

When Waylon and I left his mom, he was a mess. We tried to talk our way back into a relationship, but how? I couldn't see it. Bonnie was right. My friends were right. After all this time, I could no longer deny the truth: This man and I had nearly destroyed each other. Waylon didn't want me to leave, but I had to go. I went back to Nashville.

Sammi Smith died on February 12, 2005. I flew to Oklahoma City to attend the funeral. I was invited to sing and was honored to do so. There was an open casket. Because Miss Sammi loved to smoke, friends had filled her casket with cartons of cigarettes and bottles of her favorite coffee drink, Frappuccino. You could barely see her little head sticking out. I left the graveside and Oklahoma knowing this relationship was over.

I'm glad to report that ultimately Waylon found both sobriety and success. As of this writing, in addition to his solo work, he's a prominent singer/guitarist in Willie Nelson's live band. Just as his father, Jody, was a beloved member of Willie's tight-knit musical family, so is Waylon, a beautiful man of deep soul and tremendous talent.

CHAPTER 25

"I WILL NOT SET FOOT IN YOUR CHURCH"

THOSE WERE THE words I spoke to Dony McGuire, the piano player for the Rambos, a Southern gospel group I grew up listening to. I loved their distinct three-part vocal harmony, and I especially loved the singing of Dony's wife, Reba Rambo, daughter of the legendary Dottie Rambo.

Dony and I were speaking in a downtown Nashville honky-tonk where, during my first set, I had recognized him in the audience.

"One of my musical heroes is here," I said, "and in honor of Mr. Dony McGuire, I'd like to sing a song."

A cappella, I sang "Amazing Grace."

At the break, Dony gave me a hug. He said he had just started an affirming church in Nashville called the River. By "affirming" he meant gays were welcome.

"I love you, Dony McGuire, but I have no interest."

"Let me tell you more about the church," he said. He went on to describe a congregation that harbored no prejudice. He told me that God had spoken to his heart. That the LGBTQ community needed such a sanctuary.

I listened but was still not moved.

"Reba will be excited to see you," said Dony. "Services start at ten. Come earlier and we'll work out a song for you to sing."

"You're not hearing me, Dony. I will not step foot in your church."

"Everyone will be excited to see you, Ty. The timing's perfect. We're in divine order here."

"I wish you and Reba all the best," I said, "but I've had it with churches."

He wrote the church address on a slip of paper and handed it to me. "See you tomorrow, Ty. God bless you."

That night after seeing Dony, I didn't get much sleep. I kept thinking of the church—how I mistrusted it, how it had hurt me. I couldn't remember the last time I'd gone to church. Church was part of my distant past. I couldn't forget the hypocrisy of the conservative Christian community. Yet I also couldn't forget the joy of communal worship. I hated the homophobic bigotry but loved the music, the singing, the loving attention I had received as a little boy. But I had also received scorn. I'd been wounded by rejection. Surely the church of Reba and Dony was different, but church was church. Any church would bring back the deepest pain of my childhood, the initial trauma, the open wound.

* * *

Sunday morning, my mind still swimming, the sun shining bright. Mom made me pancakes.

"What's on your mind, son?" she asked.

"Church."

"You feel like going to church?"

"No, I don't."

"Then don't go."

"But there's a church where Dony and Reba are inviting the gay community."

"How far from here?"

"Two minutes."

"Then go."

I went.

I walked in and immediately saw Reba. My heart started beating like crazy. I loved her so much. And her church was magical. It smelled clean. It felt wholesome. What a sight! Men with men, women with women, all in full worship, all smiling, waving their arms and singing praise to God—what a revelation! I was shocked and almost giddy. Time to put shame behind me. Time to return to the fold. To travel full-circle back to where I had begun.

"Hey, son," said Reba. "Welcome home, child of God. You going to sing with me?"

"That's the reason I came."

"Let's sing 'Sheltered in the Arms of God.' You know it, right?"

"Every word."

"Then sing lead. We got you."

I got up and sang my heart out. The church was small, but the love was big. Singing gospel music made me feel good. Those hymns brought back precious memories of Grandma Myrtle's *Variety Hour*. When I was through, I was moved to give my testimony, something I hadn't done since I was a teenager. And there it was, like an old friend: my faith. I was that ten-year-old preacher boy, but this time with no judgment. No shame.

"I was lost, and then I was found, and then I was lost again," I said. "I've been born again—and again and again."

Did I come out? Did I make a public statement affirming my homosexuality? Well, no. But I didn't have to. Standing in front of this particular congregation was its own clear declaration.

Hands were waved. Hallelujahs were shouted. "Go on and preach!" rang out.

"Don't get me started," I told the congregation, "or I'll preach all day."

I stopped myself before getting too carried away. I sat down and let Pastor Reba have her say. She said beautiful things about the beautiful messages in the Bible. She talked about how she had misunderstood scripture for much of her life. She said that Jesus excluded no one.

When I got home, Mom was waiting for me.

"Your eyes are twinkling," she said. "Haven't seen that twinkle for a while."

"The River is a different kind of church."

"You felt like you belonged, son?"

"I did. Will you come with next Sunday?"

"I will."

"I can say that I'm really happy, Mom."

"That's because you're a church boy, Ty."

The River, the first congregation in Nashville to affirm the spiritual legitimacy of the gay and lesbian community, became my church home for the next five years. This was hugely important, because there was no longer any disconnect for me between being gay and being Christian. I had never lost my faith; I had just doubted that the church had a place for me. Turns out that the sacred love I felt as a child was genuine. God had never left me.

In fact, I even had a short and sweet romance with a beautiful male member of the congregation. I met him with his hands up, praising the Lord.

Was I worried that my attendance at a gay-accepting church would make the news and out me before I was ready to come out? The thought occurred to me. But the beauty of the River overwhelmed all worries. The River made me feel safe.

CHAPTER 26

RIGHT ABOUT NOW

IN 2006 I recorded *Right About Now*, my first record of new material in eight years.

I had a boyfriend I adored—David Ross, a singer and actor I'd met in LA during a visit with Tim Aldrete. I was forty-four and he was thirty-two, a proper Englishman who'd sung with Bad Boys Inc, a successful four-man vocal group. David was also a screenwriter and an actor who had recently starred in the feature film *Quinceañera*.

We bumped into each other coming out of a club. He liked my Alabama twang. I liked his British accent. He also liked country music. David had a beauty that I cherished from the moment I met him. I felt that this could be much more than a fling. I could see us together for years to come. Long-distance love affairs aren't easy, and neither was ours. I frequently flew to LA. David frequently flew to Nashville. Unlike most of my previous boyfriends, David didn't carry heavy baggage. He was all easygoing tenderness. He was as intrigued by my culture as I was by his. I felt confident that all was well.

My confidence was misplaced. As was my way, I undermined what was good in my life. I did so for reasons I did not yet understand. I thought I had it together. I didn't. I can list the "should haves" and "could haves"—could have called my sponsor; should have gone to a twelve-step meeting. This is an incident I'm tempted to skip over because it makes me look weak. Well, I *was* weak.

I was visiting David in LA. He went off to the Sundance Film Festival in Park City, Utah, where *Quinceañera* was being shown. I dropped him off at the airport on Friday. On Sunday I was set to fly to Nashville for an event, so I couldn't join him in Park City. The song says that Saturday night is the loneliest night of the week. I can't say I was lonely—but maybe I was. Maybe I couldn't stand the idea of being alone. Maybe it was the trigger of being alone in LA. My mind started going back to the old loop of getting high. Sex. Fantasizing about the red-hot combination of getting high and having sex. I thought I had thrown out the number of my drug dealer in West Hollywood. I hadn't. I could scratch out the number. I could call a friend like Tim or Donna or Bonnie. I could check in on Mom. But I did none of those things.

I got the number, made the call, and went to my dealer. Got loaded on crystal meth. I blew up my sobriety and, as it turned out, my relationship with David. I felt so guilty that I confessed what I'd done to a sober friend. The friend was sympathetic. I thought. I then flew back to Nashville. David called from Utah. So far, the film hadn't won any awards, and he was tired of hanging around the festival. He said he missed me. I suggested he come to Nashville. I had every intention of letting him know about my slip, but I figured it would be better to tell him in person. He flew to Nashville, where the next evening he learned that, after he'd left Sundance, the film had won the Audience Award and the Grand Jury Prize. So, I threw him a party to celebrate. I didn't want to ruin the fun by telling him that I'd relapsed. I would tell him the next day.

But, for reasons I still don't understand, the friend to whom I had confessed decided to report my confession to David before I had the opportunity. That was that. Understandably, David was done. He didn't look back.

That night I had a show that I managed to get through. After the last song, I walked into the wings and fell to pieces. I barely made it to the bus, where I locked the door behind me. No meet-and-greet.

The thing that put me back together was, as always, music. Lizard, who was managing me again, had introduced me to Darrell Brown, a studio wiz and renowned writer. He'd cowritten "You'll Think of Me" for Keith Urban. Darrell invited me to sing at Nashville's Bluebird Cafe, a hallowed space for country singer-songwriters. It was while performing at the Bluebird in 1988 that Garth Brooks got his first record deal. My Bluebird gig garnered great publicity. In the aftermath of that engagement, Darrell became my producer.

Man, I was ready. I needed a jolt of musical energy—and Darrell had musical energy to spare. Jolly, creative, and unrelentingly positive, Darrell was a proud, openly gay man. He spoke about sobriety and monogamy. Because he and I had discussed my history, he urged me to attend twelve-step meetings again. Those meetings were exactly what I needed.

I also needed Darrell's business acumen. He was the one who brought me back into the reality of the music business.

"You're too good a singer not to be recording, Ty," he said. "You need to remember who you are."

We lined up a label—Pyramid—and, along with Jonathan Yudkin, a top-notch fiddler and orchestrator, Darrell was the main force behind *Right About Now*. The productions were big. I hope it doesn't sound like boasting, but my voice was stronger than ever. Certain song titles intrigued me. One was called "You Still Own

Me." When I sang it, I wondered—who was I singing to? A song about obsessive love suited me just fine, but was I still caught up in my obsessive past? In hindsight, the answer is yes.

Another was called "If I Could Only Have Her Love Back," and another was titled "Hide." Yup, I was still hiding. Still not ready to come out. Still worried about losing my fan base.

A hardcore optimist, Darrell insisted there was nothing to worry about. His positive attitude came out in the last cut on the record, "There Will Be a Better Day," a tune he wrote with Beth Nielsen Chapman. (To this day, LeAnn Rimes concludes her show with that song.) Singing it felt great. And when it was time to put together the package, I felt like Gloria Swanson: "Mr. DeMille, I'm ready for my close-up."

On the cover shot, I'm wearing a T-shirt and jeans. I come off a little aw-shucks bashful. I'm thin as a rail and country as home-baked pecan pie. My smiling expression seems to say, "Right about now, isn't it time for you to accept me just as a country singer? Nothing more? Nothing less?" On the back cover photo, I'm wearing a crewneck sweater. My face is more serious. You can see how serious I am about getting back to where I once belonged.

Thanks to Darrell Brown, *Right About Now* did just that. He worked his tail off to present me in the best possible musical light. I'm proud of the album. It reestablished my presence as a recording artist in Nashville. But any hopes of busting out big on the charts were quickly dashed. The reception was quiet. I felt deflated and fell into another one of my inevitable funks. As fast as I went up, I went down again. Notice any patterns here?

Ty on the red carpet at the Country Music Association Awards, 2006.

CHAPTER 27

RESTORATION HERNDON

I WAS IN a lull. In the world of country music, I wanted more but was getting less. There was no repairing my relationship with David Ross. I was back to hooking up, but basically I was single, not a condition I easily tolerated. I was living in Nashville with Mom, trying to take some of her patience and make it my own. But that wasn't working. Impatient and restless, I decided to get back in shape by running. Running always helps me focus. On this summer morning I was running down Belmont Boulevard when I suddenly felt a spray of cold water.

"Hey there, Ty Herndon, where you running to?"

I looked over and saw a woman who looked like a young Sally Field. She stood on the front lawn of a stately mansion holding a water hose and spraying me.

"What do you think you're doing?" I asked.

"Hosing you down. With your shirt off, you're just too damn hot. Someone's got to cool you down."

"Well, ma'am, you're doing a good job."

She introduced herself as Mary Frances Rudy. She was quick to say that she knew who I was.

"Ty Herndon, I haven't heard your music in some time. How come?"

This was 2007. I explained that I had put out an album the year before that unfortunately had garnered less airplay than I had hoped for.

"I'm sure your next album will shoot straight to the top," she insisted.

At that point there was no "next album." No record deal, no big tour. No nothing.

When I asked what she did, she proudly told me, "I'm an attorney. I run my own title company."

"Good for you," I said.

I figured that was it. I met a nice lady who owned a big mansion and spoke encouraging words. But the story didn't end there.

In two weeks, she would be hosting a celebration for the Dove Awards, where many of the guests would be nominees and winners. *Would I like to attend? Well, thank you, I would.* Mary Frances knew the party would allow me to make some great connections.

When I showed up at her home for the gala event, she gave me a big hug.

"This time you've got your shirt on," she said. "How's your fitness program coming along? You still running?"

"Every day. My fitness is on the upswing."

"And your career?"

"You want the unvarnished truth?"

"Always."

"Ain't what it could be."

"And the reason for that?"

"How much time do you have?" I asked her.

"All the time in the world."

We sat in a corner while I told her just a portion of my long story. Sensing my need for help—both spiritual and material—Mary Frances made an extraordinary offer: "You're free to live in my guesthouse," she said. "It's pretty nice, if I must say so myself."

I was a bit taken aback by the invitation. We hardly knew each other. Later I learned that the invitation wasn't all that unique. Mary Frances had a reputation for aiding and abetting gay men in need. In turn, gay men christened her the Queen of Nashville.

Before I could agree to her offer, though, I had to check with Mom. I didn't want my mother to feel that I was abandoning her.

"You'll be more independent over there," said Mom. "I think it's a good move."

Before long, Mom and Mary Frances became the best of friends. Mary Frances marveled at Mom's enlightened attitude toward my sexuality. She became my guardian angel. She appeared at a time when I was dead broke. She sheltered me rent free—and in style. Her guesthouse was amazing. We added the beautifully engraved sign that adorned my quarters: "Mary Frances's Home for Wayward Boys."

I was also given full access to the main house, where she had moved her ex-husband. She did so because he was stricken with cancer; living there made it easier for their adult children to care for him. He died only a week after I met him.

I did my best to be a good guest. On a regular basis, I cooked up Grandma Myrtle's famous chicken and dumplings for Mary Frances and her children—her daughters, Laura (who gave birth to baby girl Rudy during my stay), Kim, and Rebekah, and son, John. They were all accomplished, wonderful people who accepted me with big love and zero judgment.

This was a time when I was mainly learning to love myself; no easy task. On Sundays, I was still attending church at the River, always a source of comfort. But on most evenings I was alone watching reruns of *The Golden Girls*. Yes, I live up to that one gay stereotype. After seven seasons and 180 glorious episodes, I never tired of the show. When friends ask, "Which character are you, Ty?" my answer is, "All four. I am sassy Sophia, oversexed Blanche, ditzy Rose, and dominating Dorothy." Those girls tickle my funny bone and live in my heart as real-life ladies.

On those nights when I managed to pull myself away from the television, I might go out, but with the intention of finding a casual hookup as opposed to a serious boyfriend. Only later did I learn that Laura had good-heartedly named the path between the main house and the guesthouse "The Walk of Shame." That's because Laura was amused when she spotted the occasional gentleman leaving my place at sunrise. At the same time, Mary Frances's clan heaped no shame upon me. The song that said "ain't nobody's business if I do" applied to my life while I was enjoying their hospitality.

Fortunately, though, Mary Frances did get into my professional business. I listened to her because I respected her work ethic. She was an heir to the Rudy's Farm sausage business. On her own initiative she had built up her own company, Rudy Title & Escrow, a multimillion-dollar business.

Mary Frances also loved music. As a girl, she sang with the Rudy Sisters at the Grand Ole Opry.

"Why aren't you making music?" she kept asking me when she knocked on my door most mornings between 7:30 and 8:00 a.m. "Why aren't you writing?"

"I'm not sure I have anything to say."

"You're a lover. Write about love. You're a man of faith. Write about faith. I don't believe you don't have anything to write about. I do believe, though, that you're just sitting around feeling sorry for yourself."

That hit me. She was right. I needed to write songs and reconnect with the music I loved. Mary Frances helped me do that. She introduced me to super-talented writer-producers Caleb Collins and Wayne Haun. We began the tough task of putting together a new record. The starting point was the grand piano in the Rudy living room. Mary Frances wouldn't stop hounding me until I'd written an album's worth of songs.

"You have it in you," she said. "You just need to let it come out."

Mary Frances did everything she could to get me going. She flew me out to Los Angeles to write for a week with the multi-Dove-Award-winning writer Joel Lindsey. She also underwrote my touring career. I could get gigs outside Nashville, but they didn't pay enough to cover my transportation. That's when Mary Frances got me a Southwest Airlines credit card that let me move around as needed. Mary Frances did everything she could to get me in motion.

"You're a creative artist," she kept saying. "So get creative."

I did my best. Whether I was in the mood or not, I started writing. I started moving from suppression to expression. And the expression just poured out. I wrote night and day, falling into the zone. A theme came out in a song I wrote with Caleb Collins. The song became the album title, *Journey On*:

> *Sometimes the mountains tower high above you*
> *Sometimes the current's just too fast to swim*
> *Life can carry you all kinds of places*

Journey on.
Hold your head above the water
You can weather out this storm
There's a better day coming
A better world than you have ever known

When it came time to do a video, my dear friend Tamara Dadd Alan put me in touch with Kevin Turner, a football star who had played for the Crimson Tide, the Philadelphia Eagles, and the New England Patriots. Kevin had been diagnosed with ALS (Lou Gehrig's Disease) and had started a foundation to help others suffering from the same affliction.

Kevin opens the video with his poignant story. I sing the song as I walk through the stands of an empty football stadium in between archival footage of Kevin's storied career.

Tamara and Nancy Eckert were the gutsy and loving ladies who gave me a deal on their FUNL Music record label. I very much wanted to make a great album, not just for myself but for people like Mary Frances, Tamara, and Nancy, who had backed me with love and energy. In a song called "The Rest of My Life," I wrote:

I wouldn't trade a scar to be perfect
I can't imagine this is where I slow down
I'm just getting started at coming around

"Don't Pass Me By" conveyed the same urgency:

I feel an excitement deep down inside me
Like a spark that never flamed

Maybe this searching has been the blessing
Maybe I needed time to change

A tsunami of positive energy took me back to church. And, of course, the church where I continued to feel the comfort of acceptance was the River. So it seemed only fitting that the essential faith song on *Journey On*, "I Cried Out," was a collaboration with Pastor Reba and her then husband, Dony. Not only did they write the song with me but they sang background on the record.

I cried out to the Lord
And love was His reply
I knelt before His voice
And right there in His eyes . . .
There was no shame
No mention of sin
Or bringing up all the crazy places
I had been

Much of the work for *Journey On* was done with straight and gay Christian artists who saw that I was on fire for this music and did everything they could to enhance the songs. For the first time, I felt strong as a songwriter—and also as a producer. I walked into the studio with my head held high. I knew I was making a spiritual album, and it felt important and necessary to me.

Feedback was immediate. Friends and fans rallied around me. They used words like "awesome" and "inspiring." The reviews were fabulous. *Billboard* said it was "faith outside the lines." When one of the songs I co-composed—"When We Fly," a duet with bluegrass vocalist Lizzy Long—won a Dove Award, I was thrilled. The thrills kept coming: *Journey On* was nominated for a Grammy in the Southern, Country, or Bluegrass Gospel Album of the Year category. Mary Frances, without whom none of this would have happened, threw me a big celebration party. It felt like all of Nashville came out to cheer me on. At long last, I was going to the Grammys.

But who would be my date?

The answer took even me by surprise.

CHAPTER 28

MATT

NOW THAT MY career was finally back on track, I wanted stability. I wanted a stable man. I wanted uncomplicated domestic happiness. And although my relationship history was littered with missteps, this time I was determined not to stumble. My attitude was, God bless the broken road that got me here. And also God bless Facebook, because Facebook was where I met the man I was certain would be my partner for life.

I had moved into a small condo that Mary Frances had found for me across the river in East Nashville. I loved the place because, in the aftermath of the 2010 release of *Journey On*, I was feeling self-assured. My faith was renewed, and I was ready to forge a healthy relationship.

I now know that I had generated a wild up-and-down pattern. I went from relationship to relapse to record to rewind and repeat. The relationships had been unhealthy; the relapses had been humiliating and the records not nearly as successful as I had hoped. How could I have possibly ignored that pattern? How could I not have stopped to take stock of how I was living my life?

The answer is that in the past when I felt the call of new love, the lure of a new man, reason went out the window. There was no self-reflection. I wanted what I wanted. And when I saw it, I went for it.

But things were different now. There had been a shift. I was ready. Enter Matt Collum. He was—and is—a prince. After a few quick exchanges on Facebook, we both felt the spark. We were both country boys. He grew up in the cornfields of Iowa. He was down-to-earth but also big-city sophisticated. He was a successful salesman, a pharmaceutical rep with the ability to charm the stethoscope off any doctor. Matt was also a sharp real estate investor. And, of course, it didn't hurt that he was tall, handsome, and self-confident.

I met Matt when he was especially vulnerable. He was just getting out of the painful breakup of a long term relationship. Matt was working through pain. No stranger to pain myself, we found common ground. Commiseration led to commitment. Before too long, we fell in love.

The only problem was geographic. Matt lived in Kansas City.

"Come to Nashville," I said. "I think you'll love it."

He did love it. We grew closer. We compared childhoods. I told him my story of being shamed in the revival tent. He described how he had suffered similar shame. We bore similar scars.

I loved Matt's family. They were great people who accepted me with open arms. Matt was also accepted by Mary Frances and my mom. And why wouldn't they accept him? Matt was a good listener. He was sincere and kind and able to adapt to any social circle. He wasn't overly impressed with my show-business life. And, like me, he was out among family and friends, but to the world in general he remained in the closet.

At age forty-eight I was creeping my way out, but only an inch at a time. The closet door was barely open, but I could see a beam of light shining through. I knew damn well I had to follow that light. I was a middle-aged gay man, now in a relationship with another middle-aged gay man, and wasn't it time to put all this nonsense behind me?

The answer was yes, and yet I still held back. A lifetime of working in the culture of country music had me still believing that coming out was tantamount to career suicide. I supported my dear friend country singer Chely Wright when, in this same year of 2010, she came out as a lesbian. She suffered some pushback, but the reaction was mainly positive. At the same time, Chely decided to take a five-year break from her career after her announcement. That was something I couldn't do. Something I didn't want to do.

And yet I was so in love with Matt that when it came time to go to the Grammys in LA, I asked him to accompany me. He agreed.

Ty celebrates his 2011 Grammy nomination for Best Southern, Country, or Bluegrass Gospel Album for *Journey On*.

Although I walked the red carpet alone, Matt was supportive and by my side throughout that Grammy weekend. We may just have looked like two straight-acting men dressed to the nines, but to me this was huge. I wasn't out yet.

But we knew. We knew it was coming. It was just a matter of when.

"When" was postponed for the hundredth time when, rather than face Nashville head-on and announce a fact that many people suspected, I retreated into domestic bliss. I picked up my life and moved to Kansas City, where Matt had a gorgeous home with a well-cultivated garden and a backyard pool. I could still work on weekends. I could still fly to Nashville, visit Mom and Mary Frances and record whenever the spirit moved me. The label that had signed me—FUNL—was so pleased with *Journey On* that I was urged to record a second album. I would get to that album in due time; meanwhile, I was enjoying life. I moved to Kansas City because that's where Matt made my life comfortable and, more often than not, carefree.

Summer meant camping and beach vacations. Winter meant bonfires in the cornfields. Spring meant feeding the cows on his family farm. I felt a feeling of family that brought me back to my roots in Butler, Alabama.

I craved a relationship without drama, and Matt provided exactly that. It helped that Matt not only had money but knew how to manage it. He made me feel secure.

As I returned to the studio to record, my attitude was different from when I made *Journey On*, when I felt compelled to write every song. This time around I would retain my role as coproducer but, without Mary Frances pushing me, I was content to sing songs written by others, as long as those songs expressed what I felt.

CHAPTER 29

"LIES I TOLD MYSELF"

I WAS CONVINCED there had to be a sweet spot where love and lust lived in a happy balance, but I could never find it. With Matt, I was determined to create it. My priority was the preservation of our partnership. That was my mindset when I walked into the recording booth to sing "Lies I Told Myself."

The song, written by Neil Carpenter and Neal Coty, imagines a man going back over his life. He's talking to himself, saying that he'll never get the things that he wants; he'll never find success; he'll never be free of the destructive patterns of his past. He sees them as "lies he told himself," but he's also glad he didn't believe them.

I related big-time. I'd told myself I'd always found a way to ruin every good thing that came my way; that I didn't deserve and couldn't handle happiness. But now with Matt, I no longer believed those lies.

Of course, one problem remained: I was still living the big public lie that I was straight. When it came time to shoot the video of the song, I reached out to my friend Steven Goldmann, who had shot all my previous videos. Sadly, Steven was stricken with cancer, but out of devotion to me, he directed from a wheelchair.

I saw this as my pre–coming out video. All the signs were there. As I sang, certain "lies" were written on cards: "I will never be happy." "I'm a sinner." "I'm not pretty enough." "Girls don't play guitar."

That last lie was undercut by showing Anita Cochran, a fine vocalist, playing a killer guitar solo. When I left Cumberland Heights, Anita was the first person I came out to who hadn't previously known my truth. Musical soulmates, she and I bonded and became fast friends and touring partners. There was no one else I'd rather feature in this video.

And while the video did, in fact, show two men sitting on a stoop holding up a sign that said "EQUALITY"—two men looking lovingly into each other's eyes—those men were neither Matt nor myself. They were my friends Ruben and Brad. I was only the man singing the song, and, for all practical purposes, the man still clinging to a lie that I'd stopped believing decades ago.

When I sang the song I cowrote, "I'm in Love with You," I thought about Matt. But the "you" was assigned no gender. Another song I cowrote with Victoria Shaw and Gary Burr, "I Am the Man," anticipated the day that I would no longer be a liar. But for now, the lyrics were "I am the man who learned how to lie."

Another song title summed it up best: "I Can't."

But I knew I could. And I knew I would.

"You can if you want to," said Donna Scott.

"If I can," said Carl Peoples, "you can."

"You ain't fooling anybody but yourself," said Bonnie Hadden.

WHAT ABOUT MOM?

My friends were right. I wish I could say that I immediately responded to their advice. The truth was that when *Lies I Told Myself* was released in 2013, I still needed more time to prepare myself mentally and spiritually. Matt was wonderfully understanding. It was Matt who suggested that we go to a Tony Robbins seminar.

Robbins said exactly what I needed to hear: Become your true self. Activate your authenticity, your unique personal energy. That energy will take you where you need to go. You may have already walked through fire; now it's time to walk *on* fire. Bravery is required. Let spirit lead you, not fear. Fear is a roadblock. Fear denies happiness. Push past fear.

Was my caution rooted in fear? To some degree, yes. That fear had been implanted in me from childhood. But on the other hand, caution wasn't a bad thing. There were other considerations—Matt, for instance.

"If I come out," I told him, "I want us to come out as a couple. Are you comfortable with that?"

"I can manage that."

"You can?" I asked.

Part of me hoped that Matt would say, "No, you have to protect me. I'm not out in my professional life, and I can't afford to be." Except Matt said the very opposite.

"Look, Ty, I really don't think either of us is going to be hurt professionally by telling the truth."

I wanted to believe him. Part of me did, and part of me didn't. I'd been in country music forever. I knew the culture. And, yes, I knew the culture was changing. It was 2014. The Stonewall Riots had happened fifty-five years ago. The first legal same-sex marriage had been celebrated ten years prior when two women—Del Martin and Phyllis Lyon—tied the knot in San Francisco. Within this year, all fifty states and the District of Columbia would recognize same-sex marriage.

And yet . . .

"No mainstream male country singer has ever come out," I told Matt.

"Even better. You'll be the first."

"I just don't want to be the last."

"There's no chance of that. Others are sure to follow."

And yet . . .

"And yet what?" asked Miss Peggy, the ultimate arbiter on every major decision I've ever made.

"Am I cutting off my nose to spite my face?" I asked.

"Son," said Mom, "you don't need to ask me that."

"But I am asking."

"And I'm not answering, because you already know the answer. You've known it for years."

"I wasn't ready then."

"That's why I never pushed it, son."

"But I feel like I'm ready now."

"Praise the Lord and pass the biscuits!"

And with that, I gave my mama the hug of my life.

CHAPTER 30

OUT!

NO MORE HIDING or half-stepping.

No more ducking and dodging.

No more masks.

No more smoke screens.

No more posing and pretending.

As it turned out, my caution paid off—because when I did come out publicly, I did so fully prepared to not only face the press but employ the press to put a positive spin on my decision.

Still, all the preparations didn't cancel out the visceral fear I continued to feel. I was still half certain the move would end my career. But what I finally decided was that my soul was more important than my career. I could live with a career gone bad, but I couldn't live with a diseased soul.

When I made the decision, my first call was to Chely Wright, who had paved the way by declaring her identity four years earlier.

"I'm scared to death," I confessed.

"Of course you are," said Chely. "I was too. That's only natural."

"How do I do it?"

"Thoughtfully. It will be a media event . . ."

"Oh, Lord . . ."

"Hold on, Ty. A media event is a good thing. A way to spread the good news. But you'll need experts to lead and support you through the maze. Are you coming out alone, or will Matt be there with you?"

"Matt and I are doing it together."

"Great. Let me make a call and I'll get right back to you."

Chely did as she promised. She introduced me to the world of LGBTQ advocacy, which included GLAAD (formerly known as the Gay & Lesbian Alliance Against Defamation), a nonprofit whose official aim is "to ensure fair, accurate and inclusive representation [and to create] national and local programs that [advance] LGBTQ acceptance."

The next step was to fly to New York to meet the GLAAD A-Team. When we got to the Nashville airport, I was nervous. Now there was no going back, but a small part of me still wanted to flee. Walking to the gate, I also wanted to hold Matt's hand, but I couldn't. I waited till we were seated. He knew I had butterflies and whispered in my ear, "Everything's great."

We landed at LaGuardia and went straight to meet Zeke Stokes, the GLAAD vice president, a brilliant and connected LGBTQ leader. I immediately felt safe in his presence. He was so reassuring. Zeke knew his way around the media and country music—as did my longtime publicist, Christy Walker-Watkins. She was in lockstep with my decision too.

The planning was strategic. In determining how and when, we took our time. The "how" was granting an exclusive to one print outlet—*People* magazine—and one broadcast outlet—*Entertainment Tonight*. The "when" was several months off—November 20, 2014.

Between now and then, the butterflies reigned. Mom reminded

me that butterflies are beautiful. I tried to appreciate the butterflies that had taken up permanent residence in my stomach. Despite my anxiety, I was all in on the planning. I watched the calendar as the days passed. Among the many people helping bring me peace—along with my large coterie of friends—were national figures like Mitchell Gold, the out and proud furniture magnate who talked to me for hours on end.

Before I knew it, it was November 20, and Matt and I were waking up in our midtown Manhattan hotel room. The butterflies had taken flight. I was no longer fluttery. The Holy Spirit had taken over once again. I was calm—but also excited. I showered, shaved, and felt fresh as a daisy. Matt looked like a million bucks. We were both in sharp suits. We were ready to rock.

And rock we did! A lifetime of anxiety melted away. I finally felt free. I felt like this was something I should have done decades earlier.

Ty with his future manager Zeke Stokes and Zeke's husband, Troy Cassel, at a GLAAD event in New York City in 2015.

But I also knew that "should haves" and "could haves" were a recipe for misery. All that mattered was that I was doing it now.

When I arrived at the *Entertainment Tonight* studio, my energy and goodwill were overflowing. I was a man on a mission. Lovely reporter Nischelle Turner did the interview. When she asked me about the song "Lies I Told Myself," I said, "My biggest lie was that I couldn't be gay and be in country music. Today I get to tell the world I am an out, proud, and happy gay man."

The *People* interview was super positive. I talked about how Mom had accepted my sexuality from the start and offered me nothing but unconditional love. I said, "I sit on the tailgate of my pickup truck, meditate, and talk to God. That's really all I need. I have a connection to something bigger than myself, and no one's going to tell me that I can't have it."

I also talked about the changing culture of country music. I pointed out that this year Kacey Musgraves's "Follow Your Arrow" won the CMA Song of the Year with an LGBTQ-affirming message.

The article also highlighted my history with drugs and my relationship with Matt. A photo of the two of us, smiling like we'd won the lottery, was plastered all over *People*'s website.

The story went viral. We made the *CBS Evening News*, and Deborah Norville reported it on *Inside Edition*.

I didn't have time to wonder about the reaction, because the reaction came in like a sweet summer storm. That day my phone blew up with love. I got more than three hundred text messages, all congratulatory. And as an extra bonus, country singer Billy Gilman came out only hours later, calling my announcement his inspiration.

Soon after, Chely took me to a concert featuring my friend Kristin Chenoweth and an LGBTQ choir. Kristin sang a gorgeous aria that gave us goose bumps. Backstage, she was talking to Hugh Jackman when she spotted me. In true Chenoweth fashion, she ran into my arms. "I've been waiting so long to see you, Ty. I can't tell you how proud I am of you. I just love you!" I felt ten feet tall.

So many of my friends in the business publicly and privately applauded my move in one way or another: Blake Shelton, LeAnn Rimes, Keith Urban, Tim McGraw, and Faith Hill among them. I never dreamed this decision would be met with such support.

When I got back to Nashville, I went to Waffle House to have breakfast, and a sweet old lady waited on me.

"You're Ty Herndon, aren't you?" she asked.

"Yes, ma'am."

"Well, I just saw you on TV. I loved what you said. I told my nephew all about you. I said him and his boyfriend need to learn

Kristin Chenoweth; her husband, Josh Bryant; and Ty and Alex backstage at Kristin's 2024 show in Nashville with the Nashville Symphony.

about you. What you did is gonna help a whole lot of people like you. Can I give you a hug, son?"

"You sure can. If you don't mind me crying all over you."

"Don't mind at all."

The tears kept flowing when I got a call from Charlie Daniels, a titan in country music whose numerous hits include "The Devil Went Down to Georgia." I don't know if Charlie knew it or not, but I hadn't been invited back to the Grand Ole Opry since my 1995 arrest. With one call, Charlie changed all that. Three days after I came out, he told me, "Ty, I want you on my show."

That Opry appearance might have served as a good conclusion to this book: I'm onstage with Charlie Daniels. I'm feeling the spirit of Patsy Cline. I'm singing and grinning from ear to ear. Matt is in the front row. Miss Peggy is next to him. A horde of friends are cheering me on. The crowd is on its feet. I get goose bumps. I feel relieved and redeemed. It all feels so righteous. I'm seeing the road ahead strewn with rose petals. This must be the happily-ever-after moment I've been praying for.

Or if that isn't a good happy ending, I have an even better one: Just three days after my life-changing announcement, I'm in Chicago for a sold-out show. I'm standing in the wings, about to walk onstage. My throat is dry, my knees are shaking, my heart is about to bust out of my chest. I think I'm going to faint. But I don't faint. I'm greeted by the biggest standing ovation of my career. The audience almost doesn't let me sing. They won't stop cheering. And guess what I do? Yes, that big crybaby, Ty Herndon, breaks down. Then I somehow manage to sing my heart out for more than two hours.

After the show, things get even better. In my dressing room, a family is waiting to greet me. A mom and dad are there with their fourteen-year-old, who has just come out to his family. Dad says, "My son loves country music, and especially loves your music. What advice can you give him?" All I can do in that moment is praise God for these parents. I'm thinking, *This is what unconditional love is supposed to look like.* My advice to the boy is simple: "Do what you love, and let love take you where you need to go."

Ty with the late publicist Howard Bragman, who quarterbacked his coming-out strategy in the media in 2014.

CHAPTER 31

GOD AND THE GAY CHRISTIAN

THAT'S THE TITLE of a book that was fortuitously published a few months before I came out. I ate it for breakfast, lunch, and dinner. I loved it because the author, Matthew Vines, gets straight to business when he cites specific passages—Genesis 19:5; Leviticus 18:22 and 20:13; Romans 1:26 and 1:27; 1 Corinthians 6:9; and 1 Timothy 1:10—that have been used like sledgehammers to argue that homosexuality is sin. (The Leviticus passages were the very ones used to shame a certain ten-year-old who attended a tent revival back in 1972.) Vines shows how those passages have been taken out of context and goes on to justify his subtitle—*The Biblical Case in Support of Same-Sex Relationships*—with scholarly precision and commonsense reasoning. I found it heartening, because deep in my bones, I believe that the loving spirit of Jesus is incompatible with any form of bias.

I must have bought a dozen copies to send to friends and to several members of my family whose Baptist-Pentecostal principles kept them from embracing who I truly was. I figured that as folks who studied their Bible, they might be persuaded—or at least fascinated—by the author's deep scripture-based dive. For the most part, no such luck. I could take comfort, though, in the book's conclusion that "the most powerful case gay Christians can offer is the witness of their own lives." That's what I was determined to do.

The first public witness came during that same winter of 2014, when I performed at the Trevor Project gala concert in Los Angeles. During rehearsal, I sang "Journey On" accompanied by a choir whose members were gay men and women. I remember thinking that I was no longer standing in my own shadow. My shadow self was gone. My dual life was over. I felt the other singers looking at me with the kind of admiration I had never felt before, and not just for my voice. They were admiring something I had been lacking for so long: my integrity.

Matt joined me that night. We walked the red carpet together. Matt did so with great aplomb. Dozens of flashing bulbs didn't bother him in the least. You'd never guess that this was his first red carpet. My mind traveled back to red carpets I'd walked with a woman on my arm. Whether that woman was one of my wives or a gorgeous actress like Donna Scott, I had wanted the public to see me as straight. Now, my first red carpet as Out Gay Ty Herndon was a huge deal. Man, did it feel good!

Long before coming out, I had supported the Trevor Project, an indispensable nonprofit set up to prevent suicide and help manage crisis situations in the LGBTQ community. In fact, I'd first sung at the annual Trevor concert years ago at the request of John Blaylock. I was presented as a country star, though I'm sure many in that crowd suspected my truth. This time, though, I was presented as a proud gay man. My heart burst with joy. In that audience, I saw so many faces that I knew were on the same journey.

That same joy carried over when I partnered with GLAAD's Zeke Stokes to put together the first annual Concert for Love & Acceptance on the eve of the legendary CMA Fest in Nashville. I used the same Love & Acceptance handle for the foundation I set up to help at-risk LGBQT folks. The concert got massive positive media publicity. As the years went by, it was tricky to keep the thing alive, but, in spite of serious financial challenges, we've managed to do it. In 2025, we celebrated our tenth anniversary.

I want to say that, given the beautiful reaction to my coming out, the rest of my story was smooth sailing. But that's never how life works, is it?

In that same year of many blessings—2015—I worked closely with Erik Halbig, my longtime guitarist-producer-songwriter. Erik,

Ty's manager, Zeke Stokes, with Tanya Tucker, Vince Gill, Terri Clark, and Ty backstage at the Concert for Love & Acceptance in 2018.

along with Drew Davis, another great producer, got the best out of me as we crafted an album I called *House on Fire*. I was proud to cowrite much of that album.

"House on Fire"—the first single I released after coming out—is about being a prisoner to everything. The singer is trapped; in this house of horrors he faces mirrors everywhere; he's repelled by his own reflection; he pours on the gasoline, lights the fire, and runs outside to watch the flames burn the entire structure down. Why? Because as a little kid he was told that his queer soul wasn't worth saving. Therefore, burn it down. Burn down his memories. Burn down this house.

By putting those emotions to music, I hoped to finally free myself of my feelings of self-hatred. The song was a way to purge the past, embrace the present, and face the future. I was sincere, but oh so naïve! My self-hatred and trauma went deeper. There was more to face than the memory of the Preacher in that tent revival.

The other songs on *House on Fire* were lighter fare. "World I'm Livin' In" was all about the rush of love. I saw "Stick with What I Know" as a straight-up love song. The song says that I know everything about him, but what I don't know is what I'd do without him.

The album, released in 2016, hit home with my fans. Cheryl Harvey Hill, a reviewer for NutsAboutCountry.com, wrote that "listening to the album for the first time was like meeting up with a friend and listening as he told me about his experiences." That's exactly what I wanted to achieve.

CHAPTER 32

TROUBLE IN PARADISE

IT WAS SUMMERTIME in Kansas City, and our guests were just leaving. The pool party had been fun. Baking pies and grilling steaks, I was in my element. I love feeding friends. I was proud of the beautiful home that Matt and I shared. Matt had continued to prosper as a pharmaceutical rep and real estate speculator.

Career-wise, I wasn't achieving the Garth Brooks–level of success I'd dreamt of, but I was always working, thanks to my agency deal with the world-class team at Buddy Lee Attractions. I really didn't have to worry, because money was Matt's department. From time to time, he'd hint that I needed to find a way to make bigger bucks and start investing, but I never took those requests very seriously. In retrospect, I should have. But Matt seemed happy to come to my shows and cheer me on.

This party seemed to reinforce our happiness. A big part of me wanted to legalize that happiness.

After cleaning up, we sat in the backyard. Our chairs faced the pool. The blue-lit water mirrored the moon. Fireflies darted here and there.

"Matt," I said, "what do you think about marriage?"

"I don't really think about it at all."

"How come?" I asked.

"Don't think it's really important, Ty."

"Well, it's important to me."

"I understand that, but I think things are fine as they are. Why fix what's not broken?"

"Because . . . well . . ."

"Look, Ty," he said, "I'm just not going to marry you."

That took me aback. Matt was the first man I had wanted to marry. Well, if not marriage, maybe children.

"How about kids?" I asked.

"I love kids."

"I mean us having kids."

"It's like the marriage idea, Ty. That's introducing another element that could cause all kinds of problems."

"But don't you think we could work out those problems?" I asked.

"No. And I don't want to take the chance."

"Is this a subject we might visit at a later time?"

"I don't see me changing my mind, Ty."

"Ever?"

"Ever."

Matt wasn't trying to hurt me. He assured me that he loved me. That was simply—and decisively—his point of view: No marriage. No kids.

* * *

"What about that?" I asked Mom when I called her the next day.

"Well, son," she said, "some people don't care about marriage."

"I do. We've been together forever and this is the first time I've ever mentioned marriage to Matt. This is the first time I've ever really wanted to get married. Shouldn't Matt consider my feelings about marriage?"

"Not if marriage doesn't interest him."

"Shouldn't he even think about having kids?"

"Having kids is a big deal, Ty."

"These days there are a lot of different ways same-sex couples can have kids."

"But if he doesn't want them, he doesn't want them."

"I gotta ask you the biggest question of all, Mom."

"Is the question 'Does Matt love you?'"

"How'd you know that was the question?"

"Because I know you. So sit down so I can I give you the answer."

"Uh-oh."

"No, the answer is good. Yes, Matt loves you. Matt is a loving man. Matt is a good man. But Matt doesn't love you the way you love him."

"What does that mean?"

"Your love is supersized, son. Your love can suffocate someone."

"So I'm suffocating Matt?"

"I didn't say that. All I'm saying is that you can."

"How am I supposed to pull back on love, Mom?"

"Not sure you need to."

"So everything is okay?"

"Everything is okay if you can live with someone who doesn't need you as much as you need him."

Mom's last remark hit hard. I wasn't happy hearing the word "need." I didn't want to see myself as needy. That made me sound weak. But, looking back, I know the reason I flinched was because I knew Mom was right.

Needy. I needed someone to love who loved in the same supersized way that I did.

From that point on, I could detect a growing distance between Matt and me. Feeling vulnerable, I started attending more twelve-step meetings. They always helped. But my fear about not being loved enough only grew. What to do about that fear? For the time being, nothing. Because that was a harder problem to solve than addiction. That problem ran very, very deep.

* * *

Got It Covered was the name of the album I started working on in 2018. Interestingly, there wasn't a song with that name on the record. *Got It Covered* was simply what I was telling myself. I was especially certain that I had everything covered—my personal and professional life—because I'd decided to remake the biggest hit of my career, "What Mattered Most." When I originally sang the song, I was a man singing about a woman. In the remake, I am a man singing about a man. In the recording studio, standing in the vocal booth, I loved how my history was being corrected. But here's the irony: The key line to the song—"I paid no attention to what mattered most"—was something I was still doing! I didn't want to admit that my nearly decade-long relationship was falling apart. That's because I didn't think I could survive a failure of that magnitude, after all I'd fought for and been through.

CHAPTER 33

THE MYTH OF MONOGAMY

SOME ARGUE THAT monogamy goes against nature—and especially a gay man's nature. They say man wasn't meant to have a single partner. That's just something society has imposed: Break free of society's chokehold and run free. Sure, you can have a live-in lover, a steady boyfriend, or even a husband, but you'll never find fulfillment if you don't taste the many delights awaiting you.

I didn't—and don't—buy that argument. I'm not saying monogamy is natural, and I'm not saying that monogamy is for everyone. All I'm saying is that, for me, monogamy is the easiest way to maintain a happy home. The alternate—an open relationship—results in confusion and inevitable catastrophe.

Matt and I had a good long run at monogamy. I think it felt good for both of us. But then life set in. In the long run, monogamy wouldn't save us.

Music kept me steady. Even though I still wasn't working arenas and may never do so, my new booking agency had me playing in good clubs and concert halls. I was writing material for a new album that might just get me back to bestselling "What Mattered Most" territory. What mattered most was that in 2019 I could look back at a twenty-five-year career that had proven pretty damn durable. Look at the body blows I'd survived. Sure, many were self-inflicted, but every time I found the wherewithal to get back up and keep punching. That was me talking to me. Me telling me that I was tenacious. That a bunch of my peers wanted to record with me. That my career was in good shape and my problems were in the past. That the future was bright.

* * *

While we still lived in Kansas City, Matt and I went into counseling. Maybe that would bring us closer. It didn't. What would? Moving back to Nashville.

Since I was in Nashville so often making music, Nashville would mean Matt and I would have more time together. As luck would have it, Matt's firm offered him a better position in Nashville. Great. This was all happening at a time when I was reading up on how to better manage money. Matt, who had set me up with an IRA, expected that I would be able to buy us a house in Nashville. After all, he had provided for me in Kansas City.

Mary Frances found us a cool duplex in Donelson, just outside the city. We'd live in one side and rent out the other. Great plan, except my credit was still too weak. My deal fell through. That hardly helped our relationship. Matt bought the condo instead. By then we knew that without couples counseling, we were doomed. Okay, time to find a counselor. We did. The counselor suggested we live apart for six weeks. Matt liked the suggestion. I didn't.

That six-week separation led, unsurprisingly, to a longer one. Matt and I were officially still together but living apart. I wound up alone but desperate to save my relationship, in a 750-square-foot studio apartment in the Nashville neighborhood called the Gulch.

I held on to the image of Matt and me as America's Gay Sweethearts in *People* magazine. I didn't want that image to fade. I didn't want to admit that our ten-year partnership was nearly over. I had no brain for maintaining or repairing romantic relationships. Matt had tried to teach me how to handle money, but I had no brain for money. I blamed myself for not being the man Matt wanted me to be. I blamed myself for everything. It was a familiar place for me.

I hadn't listened to Mom. I hadn't figured out how to allow Matt to be Matt outside of my dependence on him. Codependence. Add that to my ever-growing list of addictions. And then, alone and isolated, that old familiar ache came to mind:

A hit of crystal meth would give me some relief.

But no, not that. I had too much recovery. I'd attended too many meetings. I wasn't about to go back there. These boots were not walking in that direction. I'd fight the good fight.

And maybe I could have done just that, except for one thing: The world was about to go to hell in a handbasket.

CHAPTER 34

ARMAGEDDON

COVID HIT ME hard—I ultimately caught it four times—and, far worse, my career blew up in a puff of smoke. My 144-date tour schedule disappeared in the blink of an eye. I was counting on those dates to make up for the loss I took when the booking agency representing me went bust. Their bankruptcy cost me everything, leaving me in financial ruin. There would be no new record deal, no book deal, no made-for-TV movie—all things that had been in the works. Besides my pickup truck, I owned nothing but a few bucks in the bank.

I hadn't figured out how to pay the balance on my dental bill when, three days after an implant had been placed inside my mouth, I woke up, looked in the mirror, and saw that my face had ballooned up as big as a basketball. I ran back to the dentist, who said a severe infection had set in. I required an antibiotic drip. "If you get Covid again," the dentist said, "you won't survive it. You don't have the antibodies to fight it. So don't do anything foolish. Don't invite anyone in. Don't go out."

I had to go out. The rent on my studio apartment in the Gulch was going from $1,110 to $2,300. I couldn't afford it. I didn't know what to do. And then, out of nowhere, I got a royalty check—in the business we call them "God checks"—that let me rent a spacious one-bedroom in the Royal Oaks condominiums in the West End, where I would be closer to Mom. I got the deal of the century—$1,000 a month. What's more, my unit had once been owned by George Jones.

Moving in wasn't easy. Getting a moving truck was impossible. That meant a dozen trips in my pickup. Matt helped me make the move. Unrealistically, I started thinking that might mean there was a chance for us. But Matt was merely being a good guy, while I was on the verge of losing everything—along with my mind.

Life became loony. Life became a Zoom. Twelve-step Zoom meetings helped, but they weren't the same. I wasn't the same. I couldn't see Mom because she was quarantining. For the first time, I got on dating apps. I tried Grindr, but Grindr wouldn't have me. Grindr shuts you down if you get ten complaints. I got 150 complaints from men who said I was impersonating Ty Herndon.

I thought back to Cumberland Heights when I wore the sign saying "I Am a Fake." I was the fake Ty Herndon. That's how men on Grindr saw me. Men on Grindr told me to get lost. I was lost already. I was more isolated than at any other time in my life. I thought the bigger apartment would provide relief. I was wrong. The bigger apartment just became a bigger prison. As a man who thrived in the company of others, I didn't manage solitude well. The pandemic put me in a bad place.

A break came—as it always did—in the form of music. With Zeke Stokes, now on board as my manager, I bundled together a collection of Christmas classics I'd recorded long ago and released an album called *Regifted*. But I also wanted to do something new. I reached out to Kristin Chenoweth, who became an even closer friend when she began dating my guitarist Josh Bryant. Kristin and I sang a duet on

"Orphans of God," a 2006 hit by the gospel group Avalon. At a dark moment in my life, it was a beautiful experience. When it became a number one song on iTunes and the *Tamron Hall* show asked us to perform it, Zeke took pains to get a camera crew over to Nashville, where we shot my side of a two-location video with Kristin and Josh in Oklahoma. Tamron Hall featured the video on her talk show. The album was released with a second duet, the hymn "O Come, O Come Emanuel" that Waylon Payne and I had recorded way back when. Our relationship had soured, but our musical harmony was always sweet.

I tried to dwell on the sweetness of music. I spent one morning watching scraps of paper blow across the deserted driveway. There wasn't a soul in sight. Everyone's blinds were shut tight. Everyone was locked away. No human contact. It felt like the end of the world. I turned on the TV. The news was brutal. The president was talking about putting bleach in your veins. The vaccine wasn't ready. And even before it was ready, anti-vaxxers were crying foul.

Confusion was everywhere. The shutdown was happening in the world, and in me. Night after night, I cried myself to sleep. When I woke, I cried even more. My chest was tight and my throat was parched. I couldn't make a single call—not even to Mom. I was back to thinking about my meth dealer. *Don't call your meth dealer, Ty. That would not be a good idea. That would solve nothing. Or maybe it would solve everything.* Since my body was broken and my brain was broken and my heart was sure as hell broken, why not do the one thing—the only thing—that would put me on cloud nine? On cloud nine I could look down on myself and laugh.

I needed to laugh. I needed to run. I needed to listen to me and Kristin singing "Orphans of God." The answer was anything but the dope man.

But here we go. Time to go up, up, up. Find the dope man. The dope man was chill. He and his partner must be old by now. They sold meth on the side to supplement their income. Been eighteen years since I hit him up. Was he dead? Only way to find out was to drop by. Just for a chat. After eighteen years, the horse knew the way to carry the sleigh.

The dope man was there—and so was his partner. If they were old before, they were now ancient. They hadn't forgotten me. No, sir. They greeted me with hugs. We picked up the conversation as though we'd last spoken yesterday.

"Funny you should drop by, Ty," said the dope man. "Remember last time I was telling you that recipe I had for a cherry pie?"

"Indeed I do."

"Well, as fortune would have it, I baked one only a few hours ago. May I offer you a slice?"

"You bet."

The pie melted in my mouth. "I need that recipe," I said.

"You got it. Any particular reason you dropped by?" he asked, as if he didn't know.

"This pie is reason enough. I'm gonna bake one for my mom."

"You're a loving son, Ty."

"I try to be."

"Another slice?"

"I think not. Gotta watch my weight."

"You know what keeps your weight off, don't you?"

"I sure do."

"What do you say we share a little smoke?"

"I say yes."

The old dope man opened a door and pulled out the meth. He

packed it in the pipe, lit it, and passed it to me. The rocket blasted off. Within seconds I was where I wanted to be. *Oh God, this is a great. This is what I've been missing. This is what I need.*

The old dope man loved me. He felt sorry for me. He gave me a big stash to take home, and he didn't even charge me. I gave him another hug. I wanted to get out of my mind—and this stuff would let me do just that.

The minute I got home, I went for it. The binge was on. I took a towel, rolled it up, and put it under the front door. Stapled the curtains shut. Didn't want to talk to or see a soul. Just wanted to get down to business and puff my way to oblivion.

The rest is a fog. Seconds, minutes, hours, days; it didn't matter. Time stopped. I was enclosed in a methamphetamine trance. When the trance started wearing off, I hit my supply. I didn't even want to imagine the nightmare world outside my trance. As long as I lived inside the trance, I was safe. Safety is what I craved; the more meth, the safer. But then safety slipped away when the supply dwindled to nothing. Nothing was what I feared; I couldn't deal with nothing. I had to have something, but I was too exhausted to move. Too exhausted to chase after more meth. Four days of doping. Four sleepless nights. I pulled back the shades enough to see a midnight moon as I felt myself falling into a black hole of the deepest depression I had ever known. My throat was bone dry, my eyes ached, my head throbbed. My body stank. My mouth tasted of death. "I want death," I heard myself say. And I did. I wanted out. Because my self-disgust had reached the point of no return. Because I couldn't face the deadly shame of having to admit that I had slipped for the umpteenth time after pledging and promising and swearing to God Almighty and everyone else that I was, once and for all, through with this poison. I had poisoned my soul. I was poison.

In my haze I saw the son of my first cousin Dana—Josh. Josh was like a kid to me. Josh had died a year ago when he had accidentally overdosed. Josh had come to me to say that it wasn't my time. He had appeared and I felt the pain his passing had caused the family—and the pain that my passing would cause. But the pain I was feeling overwhelmed that thought. I was leaving a big musical legacy, and that was enough. I could leave this world behind. And I could do so peacefully.

I saw the red symbols on the digital clock: December 31, 2020, and the hour was nearly midnight.

New Year's Eve. The perfect time to sink into nothingness. An eerie calm suddenly overcame me.

I walked into the bathroom, took a bottle of Ambien, and dropped all twenty-seven pills into the palm of my hand.

I filled up a glass of water and was about to start swallowing the pills when my phone somehow made a call. It did so on its own. It must have, because I don't remember making that call.

The friend answered and said, "Happy New Year, Ty."

I said, "I need your help."

CHAPTER 35

THE BEAUTY OF FLOWERS

THE FRIEND "WE" called was Debbie Carroll, then CEO of MusiCares, the people who had connected me to the Cumberland Heights rehab center sixteen years ago. "We" is in quotation marks because I cannot remember looking for Debbie's number and making the call. I do remember, though, the warmth of Debbie's voice. She knew that her job was to lighten me up.

"Baby," she said, "I'm so glad to hear from you. Now you just go ahead and dump those nasty pills. It's an awful way to go. Besides, I've got a whole plan to help you."

That's all it took. I did as she instructed. I dumped the pills. Then I called Shireen Janti, another MusiCares angel, who said, "I'm thinking, Ty, that this isn't a drug problem. It's a mental health problem. I'm thinking you need the kind of help you've never had before."

Speaking to both Debbie and Shireen, I saw myself sobbing, slobbering, blabbering, and falling apart. At the same time, the Holy

Spirit gave me enough grace to hang on and listen to what they were saying. "Help" was the word they kept using. I wanted to believe that help was on the way.

Help came quickly. I didn't feel that I deserved it, yet I accepted it. Within days, Debbie and Shireen worked their magic. God bless MusiCares. MusiCares paid for me to fly to Houston and check into the J. Flowers Health Institute.

Before I headed out, I let my close friends know what had happened. Of course I called Mom. And then, my voice still shaky, I called Matt. When he heard about my dark night of the soul, he broke down crying.

"Do I need to come over?" he asked.

"I'd rather come over there. I need to see you."

"Sure thing, Ty."

I drove to the house he'd bought in Brentwood, an upscale Nashville neighborhood. I told him that he'd always be in my heart.

I could feel Matt's genuine compassion. I wondered if there could still be hope for us.

"I hope it all works, Ty," he said. "I really do."

We hugged and I left.

* * *

In Houston, I was doubly blessed: First, Flowers had a staff of super-sophisticated and loving therapists; and second, I was assigned a 24-7 sober companion who lived with me in an apartment close to the treatment center.

My companion, David Lee, a therapist with extraordinary skills, became a permanent part of my life. The whole thing was a miracle. At the lowest point of a journey filled with low points, I finally saw the light. I was treated by a team of mental health experts who, without negating the twelve-step model I'd learned and embraced at Cumberland, diagnosed me as bipolar. They also concluded that, in addition to ADHD, I also had OCD (obsessive-compulsive disorder). Incredibly, this was all news to me. Now, of course, I see the symptoms as if they were tattooed on my forehead.

David helped me understand the severity of my condition. "You may have walked through these doors," he said, "but your soul was on a gurney."

That first day I had three sessions with my primary counselor. The main topic was Matt, who was still on my mind. I spoke as if our relationship might be salvaged. I thought maybe my breakdown might bring him to me. The counselor asked whether he could call Matt to get clarity. I said yes.

"We are broken up," said Matt, "but I wish Ty all the best with his healing."

So much for my fantasy.

Hearing Matt say this hurt like hell, but at least I could no longer bullshit myself. Matt had no interest in reconciliation. Well, at least now I could focus on what was most important: my unresolved trauma and toxic shame. I carried tons of it, so much that I spent the first weeks doing more crying than talking. Before Flowers, I'd treated the symptoms without looking into the causes. At first I was afraid to travel back to the revival tent or the hotel room where I was raped or the park where I was busted. What was the point?

David and the others explained the point. He talked about the difference between secret rooms and sacred rooms. I had enough secret rooms to fill a Grand Hyatt. Those were the rooms where I had done unmentionable things that unleashed the monster of shame. The monster of shame wields self-judgment like a sword. Sacred rooms contained zero judgment. Sacred spaces allowed me to share the nightmares out loud. Sacred spaces were also safe spaces that let me process. For the first time in any recovery setting, I talked about my addiction to pornography. I was also made to see that in my relationship with Matt, I was wildly codependent—or, in other words, obsessively reliant on him to validate me. Codependency was yet another form of addictive behavior to process. Surely I had been codependent in all my relationships. The Cowboy. Suave. Waylon. Man, I had so much to process! No wonder I stayed at Flowers for four intense months.

Through EMDR (eye movement desensitization and reprocessing)—a treatment that gently led me to relive the traumas I had suppressed—I began feeling relief. It didn't come all at once, and it didn't come without pain. There were times when I wanted to run. I didn't sleep well, and my stomach was in knots. The work required an inward focus that often freaked me out. It was the specifics of those traumatic incidents that I wanted to skip over; and yet without the specifics there could be no breakthrough.

Someone once said that there's a thin line between a breakdown and a breakthrough. Maybe because my Ambien breakdown had scared me to death, I was finally ready to move into uncharted territory and go for the breakthrough.

For the first two weeks at Flowers, I concluded that if there was to be a breakthrough, I'd have to quit the music business. It was the music business—and my insane drive to succeed in that culture—that contributed to my sickness. So, no more recording; no more touring; no more songwriting. Time to get out. Time to get my real estate license and have Mary Frances Rudy set me up to sell homes in Nashville.

"Why are you talking that way?" asked one of my counselors.

"I'm just feeling like it's God's will. I tried serving God as a singer, and look where it landed me. I need to get on the other side of music."

"You'll excuse me, Ty, if I say that your concept of God is screwed up. Along those lines, I'm recommending that you talk with the spiritual advisor we've assigned to you."

"Who would that be?" I asked.

"Pastor Clint deGroot."

"What denomination?"

"Pentecostal."

"Oh, Lord," I said. "What's a Pentecostal preacher going to tell me that I don't already know?"

The answer was a resounding "Plenty!" But it took a minute. When I first met with the pastor, I had attitude. "I'm steeped in scripture," I said. "I know the Good Book backward and forward."

"Slow down there, cowboy," he said. "I'm not challenging your biblical knowledge. I'm just suggesting that we might think about the story of Jacob."

"What about it?" I asked.

"The way he wrestled with divine forces."

"I know that story."

"From what I know about you, you've been doing some wrestling of your own. And I'm wondering how those wrestling matches are going for you. You win yet?"

"I have not," I confessed.

"And you're not going to," said the preacher. "The thing about

Jacob is that he was blessed with a limp. He was blessed with disadvantages, weaknesses that turned out to be strengths. He became a leader of his tribe. And I'm seeing you in much the same way."

Pastor deGroot got deeper. He showed me that, like Jacob, every injury I had endured carried a blessing. That blessing needed to be passed on to others in the most powerful way possible. That was the power of my singing voice. Pastor Clint was so convincing that I was soon saying, "Preacher, in fifteen minutes you have single-handedly torn down the mountain I had built about quitting the music business."

"You don't even have to call it a business," he said. "Call it your music ministry."

"I've been wanting to sing and preach ever since I was a kid."

"Well, there you go. Keep thinking about Jacob and you'll stay on the right road."

Ty in Houston during his 2021 mental health recovery stay at J. Flowers Health Institute.

"As soon as I leave this place," I said, "I'm gonna cut a new album and call it *Jacob*."

I might have been getting better, but I will always be impulsive.

* * *

Other Flowers therapists also saw my spirituality as a positive. An especially perceptive counselor said that, whether subconsciously or unconsciously, I had blamed myself for every last bad thing that had ever happened to me. I needed to see what self-forgiveness might look like.

The bipolarity piece of the puzzle was also huge. I'd been mood-cycling since childhood. I just figured I was a moody guy. I had no name for it, no idea that it was a serious condition that meds could treat. Even at Flowers—or especially at Flowers—I could go from manic to depressed, depending on what happened during a session. Getting on psychotropic meds was enormously beneficial. What the hell took me so long? Well, it took as long as it took. Forget regrets.

The big thing was this: I surrendered. Surrendering was sublime. What a weight was lifted! What peace! In my head, I kept repeating the old hymn "I Surrender All." Surrender to all the treatments. Surrender to the psychiatrists and psychologists. Surrender to the fact that I had been violated all those years ago through no fault of my own. Surrender to the groups, where listening to other people had me hearing my own story falling from the mouths of others. Everyone is different; everyone is the same.

When it was finally time to leave and return to life outside Flowers, my main reentry strategy involved David Lee. David wasn't just an intellectual; he was a soul man, a recovery guru. Graciously, he agreed to be my ongoing sponsor, an unpaid position.

So, Ty Herndon, now a certified headcase, knew the full truth about himself. Finally. With the help of the beautiful folks at MusiCares and the J. Flowers Health Institute and an army of beautiful folks back home in my corner, Boyd Tyrone Herndon could breathe. The first thing he did when he got home was sit at the piano.

CHAPTER 36

MELTING ICEBERGS

WE WERE SITTING on the living room floor of my Royal Oaks condo. It was me, a songwriting friend I'd met named Arlo, singer Jamie Floyd, and guitarist Erik Halbig. I told them that we were sitting in the very space where only a few months ago I was ready to pack it in. Telling that story, I started crying—and so did Jamie. As it turned out, everyone there had lost someone dear to them in this devastating way. Depression—that feeling of utter hopelessness—entered the room and informed our hearts. The Holy Spirit practically wrote the song for us.

In melody and words, the three of them helped me tell my story in a way I never could alone. We took poetic license and used a metaphor, replacing Ambien with a gun. The song soon took form:

"GOD OR THE GUN"
I was facedown in the darkness
By myself, I couldn't change it
But there are powers we don't know

When we think we're alone
And there's nowhere left to run
Is it God or the gun?
Staring down the barrel looking up
You only get to pick one
Oh, I prayed until my heart was numb
There was an angel making a phone call
Living room floor's where I got my miracle

During this initial post-Flowers period, I wrote like crazy. With my two coproducers—Erik Halbig and Jimmy Thow—we worked overtime. I cowrote nine of the eleven songs for an album that, in keeping my promise to Pastor Clint, I called *Jacob*.

I then returned to Houston and spent eight more weeks at Flowers dealing with my love addiction, something left undone the first time around. Going back over my life and seeing how—and why—I couldn't be alone.

With another chunk of recovery work under my belt, I made it back to Nashville in decent shape. After all, a bunch of good songs were waiting for me.

Good things were happening. Zeke Stokes, the media whiz who had advised me when I came out and who was now my manager, secured a record deal and seamlessly slipped into the role of head coach of my fourth-quarter comeback. Zeke is the ultimate pro. His elbows are sharp, but his heart is soft. His management skills are superb.

Zeke wisely suggested that I go public with the end of my relationship with Matt. Since the announcement of our coming out had made a splash in *People* back in 2014, it was only fitting to reach back to

People to disclose our breakup. With Matt's blessing, we composed a statement that celebrated the good years we had together and the mutual respect we maintained for each other.

The first single from *Jacob* expressed what I'd learned in recovery. I called it "Till You Get There":

> *After goodbye there's a next time*
> *Every letdown is like an arrow to the next part*
> *To a fresh start, to the best part*
> *That you never would have known*
> *Every scar, every broken heart*
> *Is exactly what you needed, I swear*
> *But you won't know it*
> *Till you get there*

Ty and longtime friend Terri Clark in 2023. The two struck gold that year with "Dents on a Chevy," a seven-week number one hit on independent country radio that became the top independent single of 2023.

There were also fun tracks like "Dents on a Chevy," a duet with Terri Clark. Other great country singers—Emily West, Wendy Moten, Jamie Floyd, and Shelly Fairchild—joined me on other songs. The recording process was quick. We had a blast. I felt like I was back. I wasn't alone in thinking that.

Take Cody Alan, for instance. I knew Cody back in Dallas when I was Texas Entertainer of the Year, and he was on his way to becoming the face of Country Music Television. Cody was an early supporter who had no idea I was gay—and vice versa. As it turned out, my declaration of independence helped Cody make his own declaration in 2017. And now, five years later, he proclaimed for all the world to hear: "This isn't just a comeback record for Ty Herndon—this is everyone's comeback record. Every country fan can relate to these lyrics. Perfectly written for 2022!"

I was touched and humbled by what Emma Jordan wrote in Entertainment Focus: "Grammy-nominated American country music artist Ty Herndon is back with his ninth studio album, *Jacob*. With every track my heart sinks and soars to the real moments that made

Ty Herndon and CMT's Cody Alan backstage at the North Dakota Country Fest in 2024.

Herndon—the uplifting lyrics, his authenticity, the '90s country revival, and his incredible vocals."

To be understood by a critic is its own kind of bliss. Thank you, Emma.

Also thank you, Tamron Hall, for having me back on your talk show when you were discussing suicide prevention. I got to sing "God or the Gun" and tell the story behind the song.

The album and its singles were also embraced by country radio, a place where new Ty Herndon material had not been heard in more than two decades. At the end of 2023, our team celebrated when "Dents on a Chevy" became that year's number one hit on the independent country radio charts.

If *Journey On* in 2010 represented my journey back to God, *Jacob* in 2022 represented my journey back to myself. Now where would the journey go?

I remembered what my sponsor, David Lee, liked to say about such matters:

"Follow the breadcrumbs. The breadcrumbs might lead to a place that at first might not seem safe, but that's okay. Just keep following them."

I spent the better part of a year as a single, gay, and increasingly healthy man who was not looking for a relationship for the first time ever. I focused on recording and promoting the album, my tour dates, my friends, my family, and my health.

Then, it happened.

Dear Lord, let me calm myself down before I write this next chapter.

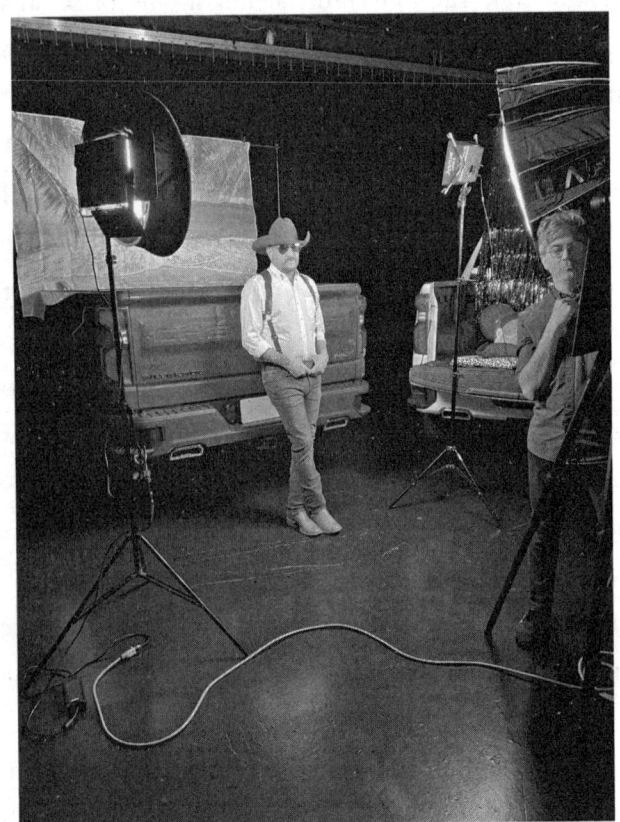

Ty on the set of the "Dents on a Chevy" video in 2023.

CHAPTER 37

"SOME ENCHANTED EVENING"

I LOVE ROMANTIC musicals. I love watching them, and I love singing those songs around the house. I love the music of Rodgers and Hammerstein. I wasn't around in 1949 when they wrote *South Pacific*, but when I heard the song "Some Enchanted Evening," I truly believed that I would, in fact, meet a stranger across a crowded room and, like magic, find my true love.

My track record erased that notion. My record could not have been worse. When it came to romance, I was Mr. Mess. Both before and after coming out, I was the King of Catastrophe. Give me a relationship with real potential and I'd find a way to ruin it. After leaving Cumberland Heights, I thought I had it figured out. Same when I left J. Flowers. But when I left Flowers the second time, I felt grounded in a hard-won reality. I was okay as I was. I didn't need a relationship to feel whole.

I still wanted to date, but dating wasn't easy, since I couldn't go on the apps. Apps were addictive. And I wasn't about to try Grindr again. To meet men, I depended on friends.

One buddy asked me over to meet a man he thought I'd like. That meeting struck me like a lightning bolt; it was the meeting that, unexpectedly and miraculously, changed everything. As I write, the memory takes my breath away.

It began with a call from a buddy who said, "Ty, I want you to meet someone special."

"I'm not looking for a boyfriend," I said. "It's been more than a year since I've chased a new romance, and I like it that way."

"I'm not talking about romance, Ty. I'm just talking about meeting a nice guy. And he's from Texas."

Texas was the magic word. "Okay," I agreed, "I'll meet him."

I was following the breadcrumbs.

When I arrived, my pal said, "Ty, meet Alex Schwartz."

The second I saw Alex, everything began moving in slow motion. All I saw were his burning brown-green eyes. For the first time in my life, someone was looking into me. He saw exactly the man I saw in the mirror. All of me. I felt wobbly, seasick. He was bathed in light. The loving aura surrounding him was almost too much to handle. I was on the verge of running out, getting into my pickup and driving home. I'm not exaggerating about this. The meeting was that intense.

Alex's beauty was spiritual; his beauty was also stunningly physical. He was muscular and lean, and his smile nearly killed me.

"Dude," I said, "you got a smile that would stop traffic."

I loved that he brought along Pipo, his Mexican rescue mutt. You can tell a lot about a man by how he treats animals. Alex and Pipo were inseparable. They seemed to share the same soul.

My friend cooked up a sumptuous meal. The conversation was

easy. Alex was super laid-back. I tried to curb my attraction to him, but good luck with that. Even in those initial moments of our first meeting, I felt drawn into his eyes. We said a lot by saying little. I felt myself pulling back. I even got dizzy. Dizzy, infatuated—call it what you will. I kept pulling back because I wasn't about to have another relationship take over my life. I did all I could to resist—and failed miserably. During that first night, love was all over me; love was all over Alex.

Alex invited me to take Pipo for a walk with him. And I did. My mind was running wild with thoughts: Alex was a whole lot more than a nice guy, although he was about the nicest guy I'd ever met. By "nice" I mean naturally kind. By "nice" I mean naturally sweet. Beyond nice, though, he felt like an old soul, as though this wasn't his first trip around the sun. He was earnest and honest. I looked for flaws. Everyone has flaws. Alex had flaws. But on that first enchanted evening, I didn't see them. I just saw his smiling eyes and knew I had to see him again. I took a deep breath and asked if we could go see a movie together the next week. I tried to hide my joy when he said, "Sure." I was skeptical—and even prayed about it—but I wanted to go for it.

A few days later, though, when I called the number he gave me, there was no ring. Wrong number. Was that Alex's way of saying "Thanks, but no thanks"? Had I misread everything?

I kept calling the number, thinking I had misdialed, but I hadn't. The number was disconnected. Alex and I were disconnected. Oh well; so much the better. I was still working on myself. Forget about that guy.

But I couldn't. Then, just when I seemed to have made peace with accepting the rejection, the phone rang.

"Hey, Ty, it's Alex. Sorry, I messed up a digit when I gave you my number. My mistake. Hope you still want to see me."

"I do."

"Well, great. When's a good time for us to get together?"

"How about tomorrow?" I suggested.

"Suits me fine."

"Come on over for lunch."

The next day when Alex arrived, we hugged like old friends.

"Hope you don't mind that I brought Pipo along," he said.

"I'd hate it if you hadn't," I said. "I love dogs. Pipo is a sweetheart."

Alex said that he'd looked me up on Facebook and was surprised that I was a well-known country singer. He loved music but didn't keep up on pop culture. Celebrities weren't his thing. I assured him that I wasn't much of a celebrity. I was from a family of pig farmers from Alabama, a country boy lucky enough to make a living making music. And if he was hungry, I'd be pleased to cook up Grandma Myrtle's chicken and dumplings. He smiled and said, "Heck yes."

After eating, we wanted a little fresh air. We both loved nature. How about Centennial Park? Great idea. We drove out there in my pickup. Pipo was happy to come along. The November sky was gray. The air was brisk. The trees had lost their green. Brown leaves carpeted the earth. Alex spoke softly. Unlike chatterbox me, Alex took a while to open up, but when he did, I could hear the pain in his voice. He was in a dark place. He talked about how he too had a history with addiction. He said he was able to confess because he'd read on the internet about my long history of substance abuse. He then spoke about the death of his baby brother—and how that loss had nearly destroyed both him and his mom.

We must have walked five miles before we stopped at a bench overlooking the replica of the ancient Greek Parthenon. We sat down to take in the magnificent sight. The setting sun turned the scene into melted gold. We were covered with calmness and peace. Alex asked whether I would hold him. I did. For a long while we stayed silent. When we got up and continued walking, I told him the stories of my many stints in rehab. When he spoke about the horrific trauma he had suffered as a child, there were tears in his eyes. We kept walking. I could feel my heart beating. I could feel Alex's heart beating as well. We reached Lake Watauga. Daylight was exhausted, and the blue water had turned dark. There were small ripples along the lake. A family of ducks glided by. The sky had cleared. I could see the quarter moon. I could see a few faint stars. I took Alex's hand. Pipo looked up in approval. We walked for another hour, sometimes talking but mostly not. We knew it without saying it: We were bonding on the very deepest level. We were understanding each other. We were falling in love. It was beautiful. It was true.

Alex stayed with me that night—and every night that week. It was clear what was happening. Ours was an intimacy I had never known before. I became Alex's safe place to land, and he became mine. All in a remarkably healthy way.

At the end of this otherworldly week, I was visited by the spirit of my father. Nearly forty years after his physical death, he appeared to me. In the past, I'd had recurring dreams where Dad and I were sitting in silence on the swing on Grandma Myrtle's porch. But now I was wide awake in the kitchen baking a cake while Alex was still in bed. I could feel Dad embrace me as an aura and hear him say, "This is good. You have my approval. You have my love." I was too stunned to move. And when I tried to sit down, I nearly fainted.

It took a while for me to compose myself. I went to the bedroom where Alex was just waking up. I told him what happened. He didn't seem surprised. He was pleased. He told me that after his baby brother had died, something similar had happened. Over a period of several days, Alex had felt the warmth of his brother's hugs.

When I told my friends about Alex, they all mentioned the age gap, yet the age gap never bothered us. Alex was quick to say, "I didn't fall in love with your age, Ty. I fell in love with your heart."

I told my sponsor, David Lee, exactly what was going on. Not only were Alex and I falling in love but we had also committed to monogamy. David suggested that we write and sign a formal monogamy pledge. We did just that.

Did I know what I was getting into? Yes. I was getting into something incredible. Given my track record, was I sure? I was positive. The positive energy between Alex and me was off the charts.

Taking Alex to meet Mom was the final test. We sat around and drank coffee. For an hour, Alex and Mom chatted like old friends.

That night Mom called and said, "This is the first person you brought through my door who looked at you the way your dad looked at me. Alex loves you, Ty. Now don't you go and mess it up."

"Yes, ma'am."

Alex had a natural charm with Miss Peggy. He snuck off to her place to watch football, bringing her a six-pack of Miller Light. That was yet another reason I adored Alex. He knew the way to a guy's heart was through his mom.

Because I'd given my heart away to so many people who hadn't taken care of it, you'd think I would be worried. I wasn't. Alex gathered all those pieces, put them together, and gave me back a whole heart.

This felt nothing like the way I'd rushed into past relationships. This was entirely novel for me. There were no precedents. There was a maturity about it. A calm certainty. But it was the crashes of the past that led me to know that critical difference. What Alex and I shared was mature. It was romantic and charming, yes. And yes, I couldn't stop thinking about him. And yes, there was a dizzy, delicious feeling of chemistry and discovery. But the core of what drew me to Alex was rock-solid. This was a love of the highest seriousness.

For Thanksgiving, Alex invited me to his family's dinner. Naturally, that made me a little jittery. When I walked inside, his mother was standing at the door.

"Ty Herndon!" she screamed.

"Charlotte Medley!" I hollered back. Alex had told his mom that he was dating a "Tyrone." Thus the surprise. Charlotte and I knew each other from the River, the church where I had renewed my faith. Talk about breadcrumbs! We had worshipped and sung together.

"I've seen you run the aisles," she said. "I know the Holy Spirit lives in you."

Within three months Alex had moved in and we were engaged. All the while, he bought and restored mid-century furniture. He also earned a full scholarship and got his bachelor of business administration degree.

The formal engagement ceremony took place in Bakersfield, California. I fell to one knee to ask Alex's hand in marriage. Then Alex did the same. After my gig that night, we drove to see Donna Scott in her Hollywood Hills home. We told her we wanted to go shopping for engagement rings. "Rodeo Drive!" she exclaimed. "Girl," I said, "Rodeo Drive is way out of our price range." "Boy," she said, "my jeweler owes me all kinds of favors." Yes indeed,

Donna's Beverly Hills jeweler gave us a deep discount. We exchanged matching rings. *People* magazine helped us announce our news to the world. We were properly betrothed. But who wants to be simply betrothed? Let's get married.

It happened on January 6, 2023. The setting was the East Nashville loft of photographer Jeremy Ryan, my good friend in all things creative. I'd shot four album covers in Jeremy's loft. In this same space, two months before marrying Alex, I had officiated, along with Pastor Melissa Greene, at the wedding of my niece Heather and her bride, Kaylee. It's worth interrupting my story to tell Heather's:

The Pentecostal branch of my family back in Alabama did a number on Heather and Kaylee. They said they supported their relationship and invited them to church. During the service, they invited the ladies up front, where a prayer circle was formed. The prayer was fine until the pastor turned to the two women and asked God to

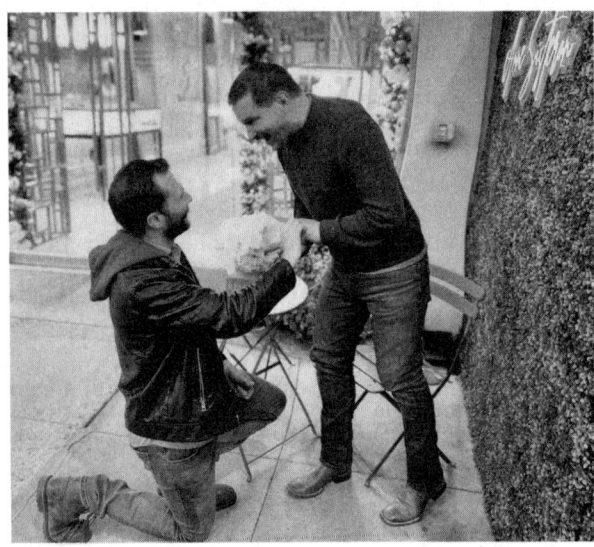

Ty and Alex make the engagement official. Beverly Hills, December 2022.

remove their diseased desire for each other. Heather, a gorgeous gal and a gun-toting, camouflage-wearing badass, told the saints "No thank you" with some choice words. She and Kaylee stormed out. There'd be no praying the gay away for those two. After that incident, one family member even accused me of turning Heather gay. So you can understand why Uncle Ty was pleased to preside over the holy matrimony of these two wonderful women.

The divine Pastor Greene also presided over Alex's and my wedding. Our ceremony was secret for good reason: We didn't want our moms to know, because we'd told them that we were planning a full-on wedding with three hundred guests in August where they'd both be honored. And you don't want to disappoint Miss Peggy or Charlotte. That was the absolute truth. Another truth, though, was that Alex and I simply didn't want to wait. Yes, we were wildly enamored with each other; but we were also enamored of the idea of being husband and husband in the eyes of God. With our marriage contracts inked, there

Ty officiating his niece Heather's wedding.

was simply no reason to wait. In our eyes we were already spiritually married, so we just wanted to seal the deal.

Miss Bonnie Hadden and Alex's brother, Aaron, were witnesses. The ceremony was brief but glorious. The groom kissed the groom, and all was right with the world. Time to move on to the big ol' splashy event. Let the planning begin!

All credit for the fabulous wedding goes to Miss Bonnie, Zeke Stokes, and Jeremy Ryan, who worked their tails off to do it right. We went for it all—tuxes, groomsmen, bridesmaids, corsages, boutonnières. We found a spot in the country outside Nashville, Owen Farm, that boasted about being "nestled on 125 acres of middle Tennessee landscape with a backdrop of the beautiful Cumberland River."

Mr. Owen had never hosted a gay wedding before, but made it clear that his venue was open to everyone. The property was adjacent to the

Ty and Alex with Alex's mom, Charlotte, at their wedding rehearsal in August 2023.

farm of Don Williams, my dad's favorite country singer. Don's touring bus was sitting on Mr. Owen's lawn. Mr. Owen thought it would be a great idea if our wedding party arrived in the bus. *Yes, sir! Let's do it. And let's go one better: Let's exit the bus while the guests are listening to Don Williams's "I Believe in Love," my dad's favorite song.*

Bonnie handled the 346 invitations and secured the perfect down-home caterers. Pork chops and gravy. Apple pies and chocolate cakes. Three-decker wedding cake with two distinguished gentlemen on top.

The big day arrived. Saturday, August 26, 2023.

What could go wrong on a hot August afternoon in Tennessee?

The weather, of course.

An hour before the late afternoon start, it didn't rain; it poured—a biblical thunderstorm hit Owen Farm. Running from their cars, guests got drenched as they sought shelter under a shed. The wedding party didn't know what to do. I was about to lose it. This was supposed to be a picture-perfect day, a picture-perfect wedding. Alex stayed steady. "I'm not marrying the weather or these people," he told me. "I'm marrying you." My man was calm, cool, and collected. I followed his lead.

Miss Bonnie saved the day by shouting out, "Open the bar!" Let the guests get a little loose. We had all sorts: sober folk, drinking folk, folk from every walk of life, famous folk (singer Kristin Chenoweth, actress Sally Struthers), families on both sides. It was an all-inclusive affair. After a while, when it looked like the rain wasn't going to stop, we got started. As the tour bus carrying the wedding party pulled up to the pavilion, I flashed back to the revival tents of my childhood. Only this was different. This was an epic celebration, an Oprah Winfrey special meets a magical Disney moment. Pipo walked next to his master as if he were his best man. Our mothers—Miss Peggy and

Ty, Alex, and Pipo at their wedding.

Charlotte—were seated behind us. Pastor Melissa Greene married us again with a message of enduring love. We had written vows to each other that, through tears, we spoke proudly. On a table I placed a photo of my dad and Alex placed a photo of his baby brother. Our mothers came to the table to light a unity candle, signifying the joining of the Herndons and the Schwartzes. Candles were lit; songs were sung. Then the rain passed and we danced the night away.

A week later, Alex and I were in Dallas to attend the marriage of Kristin Chenoweth and Josh Bryant. And we danced the night away a second time.

Just married.

CHAPTER 38

LETTING GO

COULD I?

Would I?

The one threat to our marriage was a two-letter word: me.

I knew from the beginning that I wasn't going to be the hero of my own story. But a hero did emerge: Alex.

The challenge was my compulsive nature, which, fueled by insecurity, was still on full blast. That nature was always capable of overturning the apple cart. My ADHD was raging. So was my OCD. In our home, I needed everything to be in place. The kitchen counter wiped clean. No dirty dishes in the sink. No dirty underwear on the bedroom floor. The neat-freak monster inside me was no minor character. He could emerge at any moment and go bat-shit bananas. Even though I knew of my issues and was doing the work to manage them, these were strong urges I had lived with for decades. Old habits die hard, they say.

During our first year, Alex and I were together nearly every day. Then came the big test: How would I do on the road with Alex back home? Well, not great. I worried about where he might be. I wanted to track him on my phone. I wanted to check on him every two hours. Yet I knew that to do so would drive him nuts. To do so would indicate that I didn't trust him. To do so might drive him away. So, more recovery meetings, more reflection on the depths of my fears and their relationship to my faith. More listening to that still-silent voice saying, "Take your fears, throw 'em in a sack, and leave 'em at the foot of the cross."

Prayer brought calmness, but calmness didn't stay for long. The battle between faith and fear was ongoing. I worked hard on confessing my frailties to God.

Alex did the same. He struggled mightily with the deep traumas from his distant and recent past. But the Schwartzes are very private people. For him to delve into those traumas with a group of mental health professionals over an extended period of time—well, that was foreign to how he was raised. Yet the more we talked and the more I shared my own history, the more Alex saw the need. Having been through it myself, I knew it was scary. Reliving the worst moments of our lives requires strength. We avoid going there for good reason. Who wants to rattle around in the darkness? Who wants to speak about what has always been unspeakable? Alex's decision to take on his traumas was brave. His decision to check into an in-patient treatment center in Ocala, Florida, for six weeks reinforced my view of Alex Schwartz as a man with a deep and serious soul.

While he was gone, I realized that, for all my effort, I still hadn't mastered the fine art of being apart from the one I loved for long periods of time. I hated how alone I felt. I hated how my mind went to worst-case scenarios.

As I stood in our kitchen and tried to get myself to prepare supper, I began asking that dreaded question: What if trauma therapy opened up insights that turned Old Alex into New Alex? And what if New Alex didn't love me the way Old Alex did? What if New Alex suddenly realized that Ty was too old? Or too hyper? Or too obsessive? What if New Alex decided that our marriage was too sudden, too impulsive? Would New Alex, a more emotionally healthy human being, see Ty as the wrong man for him? And yes, following breadcrumbs led me to Alex; and yes, following breadcrumbs led Alex to trauma therapy; but now will those breadcrumbs lead Alex to leaving me?

After Alex had been in treatment for three weeks, I couldn't help myself. I had to see him, and fortunately, the treatment center allowed the visit. Alex also invited his mom, Charlotte, to accompany me on the eleven-hour drive from Nashville to Ocala. That's when I got to hear Charlotte's full story. It's her story to tell, and I'll only say that she is a remarkable lady, a survivor, a fine author (the book about her child who passed is called *The Upside of Downs*), and an equally fine singer-songwriter. As I focused on Charlotte, I felt my paranoia lessening. Yet I wouldn't be completely calm until I saw Alex. I broke down and had to pull over to the side of the road. Charlotte took my face in her hands and said, "I know my son. He loves you, Ty. But remember—this trip isn't about you. It's about Alex."

Of course Mother knows best, and Mother was right. When we arrived, Alex greeted us looking like a new man. He was full of light and love. Sensing my insecurity, he was quick to say that, more than ever, his commitment to our union was unwavering. I sighed, exhaled, and took him in my arms.

Three weeks later, Charlotte and I were standing at the Nashville airport holding a sign that said "Welcome home!"

"You'd think I'd been gone for a year," Alex later recalled, "but I loved seeing the sign anyway."

Therapy brought us closer. Together, we viewed our histories with neither regret nor shame. The triumph of love wasn't inevitable, but it was possible because we both shared a clear intention: to get well. On a daily basis we committed to work hard for that wellness. Wellness meant dealing with fear and understanding that fear is in the abstract. In the now, all is well.

Ty and Alex, 2023.

CHAPTER 39

THE NOW

HERE'S THE GOOD news:

I'm feeling strong. I'm singing and recording new songs that feel deeper and truer than anything I've ever sung. I'm feeling like an open channel. Let the love come through. Let the music reveal who I am. Let the sound of my voice be of comfort. Let me sing you into love.

Let my Foundation for Love & Acceptance help heal hurting hearts. Our annual concerts have been super successful, and our public supporters include Reba McEntire, Tanya Tucker, Vince Gill, Mickey Guyton, Dennis Quaid, and dozens more.

The initiation of my podcast, *Soundboard*, was another blessing. The format allowed me to conduct in-depth interviews with, among others, former Nashville mayor Megan Barry, LeAnn Rimes, gospel great Crystal Lewis, and Cody Alan. Their stories touched on subjects that matter to me: personal integrity, spiritual growth, and how to stay sane in an insane world.

It's been thirty years since "What Mattered Most" went to number one. I hope I've got thirty more years in me. I know I ain't slowing down. I'm more excited than ever, because that ten-year-old boy who was freaked out by the Preacher is freaked out no more. That little boy who wanted to testify and sing freely and joyfully is doing just that. Now every time I sing onstage, I feel connected to that boy. He is no longer afraid. He is alive and redeemed. He lives within. The boy and the man are now one.

* * *

At the very beginning of this book, I said that I'd love for you to love me. I still say that. But the difference between where my story started and where it will now pause is this: With Alex, I've finally found the sweet spot, a sacred space where romantic and spiritual love live in harmony. That love is sufficient.

I am home. Home is where I fry up a batch of chicken. It is where

Ty's triumphant return to Billy Bob's Texas in 2024.

Alex and I entertain our circle of precious friends. Home is where I sew curtains and write songs. It's where I rest my head. Where I look over and see my husband resting peacefully. I kiss his eyes and caress his cheek. I fall into an easy sleep. And if the Nashville night is stormy and distant thunder awakens me, I slip out of bed, and walk out to the patio of our home. I look out at the twinkling lights of the city. I look up at the low-hanging clouds racing over a full moon. I breathe in the cool night air. Lightning bolts streak the sky. The energy crackles. I'm overwhelmed by all I see and all I feel. I'm excited to silently sing a song that says I'm a spirit born of God. It's a soaring anthem that declares God lives inside me, inside Alex, inside you, inside everyone. There is no separation. There is only God.

I thank God for that knowledge.

I thank God for giving me the heart to write my story.

I thank God for everyone who has blessed me by reading my story.

I thank God for everything.

Amen.

ACKNOWLEDGMENTS

To my cowriter, David Ritz—thank you for bringing my thoughts, words, and history to life so vividly. You helped me make sense of my story in ways that years of therapy never did. I am forever grateful.

To my editor at Dey Street, Carrie Thornton—I knew from the moment we met we would work really well together. What I didn't expect is that you would become a new member of my chosen family. Thank you for believing in me, guiding this process, and snatching me back to reality when I got too much in my head.

To my book agent, David Vigliano—Thanks for reading that *People* magazine story in 2022 and realizing there was more to tell. You've become a great friend, and you make a dang good marinara!

To Jason Sheeler at *People* magazine—Thank you for writing the story that got David's attention. The care you took with telling such a personal and painful chapter of my life meant the world to me.

To my manager, Zeke Stokes—Thank you for sharing the vision for this book and seeing the path to make it happen. There is a time and place for everything. I was finally ready to tell this story, and you made it happen. All my love to you and Troy!

To my longtime musical collaborator Erik Halbig—Thanks for sticking with this country music singer through feast and famine. Your talent is matched only by your heart. Thanks to you and your beautiful wife, Andrea, for decades of friendship and support.

To the dynamic producing and songwriting duo Jimmy Thow and Jamie Floyd. I'm honored to have you in my musical family. You brought so much truth to my story through with your heart, talent, empathy, and authenticity.

To Christy Walker-Watkins, Taylor Dickens, and the entire team past and present at Aristo Media for helping tell my story and share my music with the masses.

To Chris Willman, who helped me write my first book proposal a decade ago—you were ready, my friend, but I wasn't there yet. Timing is everything, and I thank you for taking that first step with me.

To Sharon Terrell, who has shown me some of the truest friendship I have ever known. Your unflinching honesty and integrity have taught me how to be a better person in life and relationships. Thank you for believing in this book more than a decade ago. (And thank you for helping me develop my B.S. detection abilities! You are epic!)

To Sharon, Wayne Hahn, Joel Lindsey, and the entire team at my new record label home Club44 Records—Thank you for believing in this phase of my career journey and helping me put out some of the best music of my career.

To Tamara Dadd Alan, who has been everything from my lawyer to my manager, to my record label head, to my Foundation For Love & Acceptance director over the years—Thanks for all that—but most of all, thank you for being a loyal friend. Everyone deserves someone like you in their life.

To Nancy Eckert, my lawyer and friend—Your heart is unparalleled, and your brain has kept me out of trouble more times than I will ever even know!

To Mary Frances Rudy—I thank God every day for that run down Belmont Boulevard in Nashville. You and your water hose changed my life for the better that day. I am eternally grateful that you are my friend. Your wisdom and love and investment in me was the beginning of my journey to believing in myself. To put it quite simply, I love you.

To Bonnie Hadden—I'm so grateful my tooth broke that day in Augusta, Georgia, and we became fast friends. Your unconditional love and support has been nothing short of a miracle in my life. You are simply an angel, and I love you.

To my best friend in this life, Carl Peoples—Thank you for standing by me when times were tough and for giving me that tough love to match. You are the brother I never had, and I cannot imagine being on this journey without you. You are highly favored, adored, and loved.

To Donna Scott—You were there for all of it, and you're still by my side as a dear friend, confidante, and counselor. Thank you for seeing me even when I couldn't see myself. You are an angel of love.

To Jeremy Ryan—Your artistry, including this book cover, has captured not just my image, but my spirit. Thank you for years of friendship, collaboration, and for always helping me shine.

To Chely Wright—Thank you for blazing the trail for me and so many others and for encouraging me to write this book. Your friendship and wisdom have been a guiding light for me. Remember that day in New York, you said to me, "you need to do a book"? Well, you were right. And I love you.

To Debbie Carroll—"There was an angel making a phone call . . ."—You were and are an angel to me and so many. Thank you for believing in my ability to achieve wellness and using your vast resources and never-ending supply of empathy and understanding to help me get there. Honestly, I would not be here today without that mystical phone call. I love you.

ACKNOWLEDGMENTS

To Dr. James Flowers, Michael Beard, Shay Butts, Melanie Somerville, Shireen Janti, and the entire team at J. Flowers Institute in Houston, Texas—Thank you for giving me the love, the answers, and the tools I needed to achieve the peace and wellness I had been searching for my whole life.

To Dena Davidson, Bubba McNeely, and Mark Lowry—Thank you for the meals, the music, and the tremendous love you showed me during my stay at the "compound" in Houston, Texas. (Bubba, we miss your light already!)

To my sponsor, David Lee—Thank you for never letting a call go unanswered and for guiding me through this thing called life, recovery, and wellness.

To my husband, Alex—Oh, the roads we both traveled to finally find each other when we least expected it. Your love and support through the writing of this book and these last three years has gotten me through. Thank you for believing in me on those days when I didn't believe in myself and for pushing me to be a better person every moment we're together. I love you deeply and eternally.

To my sister Alicia—I have loved you since I held you the first time when I was just one-year old. That will never change. I love you so very much.

To the indomitable and unflappable Peggy Herndon—Miss Peggy—Mama Peggy—You are the rock that has never faltered. I am proud of you and proud to be your son. Your love, confidence, and common sense have sustained me. I literally would not be here without you.

To my Guardian Angels—Dad, Grandma Myrtle, Grandma Inez and Grandpa Wesley, Aunt Bennie Sue, Aunt Greta, Aunt Lilly, Earl, Violet, Jewell, Inez, Laurice, Henry, Doris, Opal, Lance, Josh,

Bubba, and Wes—Thank you for shining down upon me with your light and wisdom from above.

To my Higher Power—there are no words to describe the grace you have shown me. Thank you for seeing me through all of it. I stand in awe of you. Hallelujah and amen.

And to you, the reader—Thank you for taking the time to read my words. I hope in some way you have seen a bit of yourself or someone you love in my story and that your heart and mind are bigger and open wider as a result. Be the hero of your own story.